TRIMMING THE TREE

GIFTS FOR GIVING

Crafts

DECK the HALLS

a TREASURY of CHRISTMAS CRAFTS

CREATIVE
PUBLISHING
international

Copyright© 1997 Creative Publishing international, Inc.
5900 Green Oak Drive, Minnetonka, Minnesota 55343 • 1-800-328-3895 • All rights reserved • Printed in U.S.A.

CONTENTS

AROUND THE HOUSE

AROUND THE HOUSE

Nothing is more inviting
than a home filled with holiday
spirit and joy. Deck your halls in
Christmas cheer by creating
and displaying one or more of
our unique seasonal projects.
Whether stenciled or stitched,
quilted or painted,
our clever florals,
wall hangings, stockings
and home accents will create
just the holiday look you desire.
We guarantee these wonderful
creations will light up
every room in your home!
With a little work and a lot of
love, a handcrafted Christmas
can be yours this year and
for years to come!

LUMINARIES

Holiday luminaries placed along a driveway, walkway, or outside a front door are a warm way to welcome guests to your home. By placing a light-colored bag inside a dark-colored bag with a holiday motif cutout, you can create a wide variety of patterned luminaries.

MATERIALS

❋ Mat board or piece of heavy cardboard; mat knife

❋ Dark-colored paper bags

❋ Light-colored paper bags

❋ Cookie cutters or stencils

❋ Sand, votive candles

❋ Paper doily (optional)

❋ Miscellaneous items: pencil, glue stick, markers

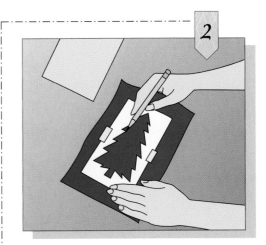

If you know someone who is planning a holiday party, delight them with an assortment of these simple, festive lights.

1 Cut a piece of mat board or cardboard so it will fit inside dark–colored paper bag. The board will protect your work surface and prevent you from cutting through both sides of the bag.

2 Trace designs or words on the dark bag using cookie cutters or stencils as templates; trace with a pencil.

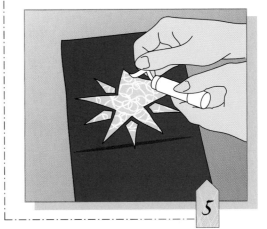

3 Insert mat board or cardboard into bag; cut designs out of bag with mat knife.

4 Remove mat board from bag. Insert light bag into dark bag, and unfold. Fill bottom of layered bags with sand; nestle candle in sand in bottom of bag.

5 If desired, cut a paper doily slightly larger than the cutout design on dark bag. Edges should not be ragged, because their silhouette may show through bag. Secure doily to inside of dark bag so that it is centered, using glue stick.

For a confetti-like look, use colored markers to make spots on light bag. Cut out holes in dark bag to reveal spots.

winter WELCOME POST

Welcome winter and all those who come visiting with a seasonal greeting of "Let It Snow!" Stencil the word "WELCOME" on a post, nail a wood square to the top and bottom, and glue on the tree and snowman cutouts. Finish off with a good sanding to achieve a weathered look—or in harsher climates, simply put the post outside for the season.

MATERIALS

❋ Wood: 4" x 4" (10 x 10 cm) post, 3-ft. (7.5 cm) length; 2" x 8" (5 x 20.5 cm) pine: 7" (18 cm) squares, one each for base and platform; 2-ft. (0.6 m) length for figures; 1/4" (6 mm) birch plywood, 6" (15 cm) square; 3/8" (1 cm) dowel, 9" (23 cm); 3/16" (4.5 mm) dowel, 2" (5 cm)

❋ Acrylic paints: ivory, white, black, forest green, red, green and rust

❋ Iridescent textured snow paint

❋ Paintbrushes: 1" (2.5 cm) sponge; No. 1 script liner; No. 3 round scrubber; 1/4" (6 mm) stencil

❋ 2" (5 cm) alphabet stencil

❋ Tools: jigsaw or hand saw; scroll saw; hammer; drill with 1/16", 3/16" and 3/8" bits; wire cutters; hammer

❋ Nails: 1 1/2" (3.8 cm) spike; 2" (5 cm) with flat head, four

❋ Wires: 18-gauge black, 3-ft. (91.5 cm) lengths, two; 24-gauge floral, 24" (61 cm); barbed, 11 ft. (3.38 m)

❋ 4" (10 cm) twigs with branches, two

❋ 2 1/2" x 20" (6.5 x 51 cm) wool plaid for scarf

❋ Artificial greens, 6" (15 cm) sprigs: pine, eight; holly with berries, two

❋ 1 1/2" (3.8 cm) red velvet ribbon, 2 yd. (1.85 m)

❋ Natural raffia

❋ Glues: thick white craft, dual-temp glue gun

❋ Pattern sheet

❋ Miscellaneous items: tracing paper, pencil, graphite paper, stylus, ruler, medium-grain sandpaper, tack cloth, disposable palette, palette knife, used toothbrush, paper towels

Preparation: Trace the four patterns. Use the graphite paper and stylus to transfer to 2" x 8" (5 x 20.5 cm) pine, and cut out. Sand rough edges of all wood, and wipe with tack cloth. Refer to the patterns to drill holes in the tree, snowman, snowflakes, and sign. See the illustration to drill holes in the 7" (18 cm) square platform.

1

2 Refer to page 158 for Painting Instructions. Refer to pattern and photo as needed while painting. Basecoat all sides of post with two coats of ivory, and platform and base with two coats of forest green. For a weathered look, sand all surfaces until the wood grain begins to show through. Stencil "WELCOME" down front of post with black paint and stencil brush. Begin 13" (33 cm) from the top, and leave about 1" (2.5 cm) between letters.

3 **Post Assembly:** Turn post upside down, and center base on post bottom. Attach with two 2" (5 cm) nails near the center. Turn post right side up. Repeat for platform; make sure drilled holes are facing up.

4 **Platform Preparation:** Basecoat the tree with two coats of green. Basecoat the sign and snowflakes with two coats of white. Lightly sand edges. Paint "LET IT SNOW!" using thinned black paint and liner brush. Cut 4½" (11.5 cm) of the ⅜" (1 cm) dowel and paint forest green. Glue in hole at bottom of sign.

5 **Snowman:** Basecoat body with two coats of white and hat with two coats of black. Float white along hat brim to shade. Add three holly leaves to hat using green. Dot red berries at center. Use end of ⅜" (1 cm) dowel to make eyes and buttons with black. Dry-brush cheeks with scrubber brush and red paint.

6 Cut a 1½" (3.8 cm) piece of 3/16" (4.5 mm) dowel and sand one end to a point for nose; paint with rust. Glue into nose hole. Glue twigs into arm holes. Paint mouth and eyelashes with thinned black paint and liner brush. Use liner brush and thinned white paint to add comma stroke highlights in eyes. Clip ends of wool scarf to fringe; tie around snowman's neck.

7 **Platform Finishing:** Dip bristles of toothbrush in thinned white paint and spatter all sides of tree, snowman, sign, and snowflakes. Cut two 2" (5 cm) pieces of ⅜" (1 cm) dowel and glue into bottom holes of tree and snowman. Glue tree, snowman, and sign into appropriate holes in platform. Use palette knife to apply textured snow accents, as desired, to figures and platform surface. Tie a raffia bow around the sign post.

8 **Barbed Wire Wreath:** Bend and wrap wire into an 8" (20.5 cm) circle. Align the two lengths of 18-gauge wire, then bend in half and twist together to form a 1" (2.5 cm) loop hanger. Position hanger on back of wreath; tightly wrap wire tails once around wreath, leaving ends in front. Beginning close to wreath, coil half of a tail around a pencil; string on a snowflake and twist wire to secure. Coil remainder of tail around pencil. Repeat to coil all tails and attach snowflakes.

9 Use floral wire to wire artificial greens to wreath. Hot-glue a raffia bow to wreath. Make a six-loop red velvet ribbon bow; wire and hot-glue on top of raffia bow. Hammer spike nail to post front, 3" (7.5 cm) below platform. Hang wreath on nail.

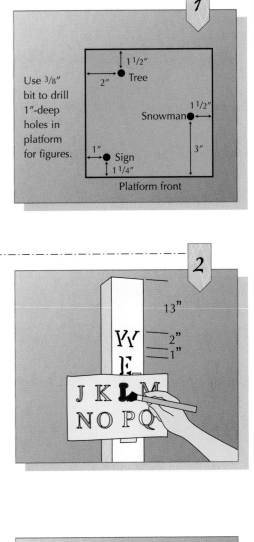

CARDINAL DOOR DECORATION

Our front door decoration has a clever cardinal perched on a cinnamon stick amidst painted wooden embroidery hoops filled with greenery, berries and tiny pinecones on a red and green plaid bow. This cardinal will remain a bright, cheery spot of color all through the winter, or for as long you keep him up. And, unlike the real thing, he won't fly away as guests approach your door.

MATERIALS

* 4" (10 cm) wood embroidery hoop
* Metallic gold acrylic paint
* Small hobbyist paintbrush
* Hot glue gun
* 2½" (6.5 cm) artificial cardinal
* Cinnamon stick, 3" (7.5 cm)
* 4" (10 cm) artificial evergreens, 12 sprigs
* Red wired holly berries, 24
* ¾" (2 cm) pinecones, nine
* 30-gauge green cloth-covered wire, 6" (15 cm)
* 1⅜" (3.5 cm) red/green plaid ribbon, 1 yd. (0.95 m)
* ¼" (6 mm) red satin ribbon, ½ yd. (0.5 m)
* Miscellaneous items: scissors, wire cutters, ruler

1 **Hoop Cage:** Separate embroidery hoops, and paint each one gold. Let dry. Refer to the photo for all decorating and assembly steps.

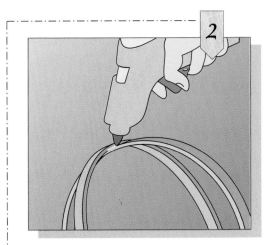

2 Slide the smaller hoop inside larger one. Position at right angles; glue where hoops touch. If hoop has screw, assemble frame, apply glue, and tighten screw. Position screw at bottom to complete project.

3 **Decorating:** Glue the ends of four evergreen sprigs at inside bottom hoop intersection, allowing a sprig to extend from each quarter section. Repeat to glue four sprigs to outside bottom hoop intersection. Glue three sprigs on outside top hoop intersection.

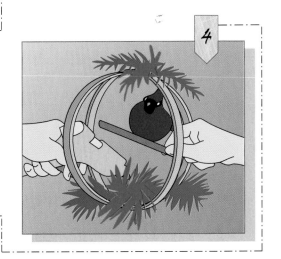

4 Glue the cardinal to the cinnamon-stick perch, then glue perch to center of greens. Randomly glue three pinecones and seven or eight berries, in clusters or singly, among greens. Cluster remaining pinecones and berries, and glue to center top greens.

5 **Finishing:** Form a 6" (15 cm) two-loop plaid bow with 5" (12.5 cm) streamers. Wire bow center and cut V's in streamer ends. Glue bow to center of bottom greens.

6 **Hanger:** Overlap ends of ¼" (6 mm) red satin ribbon inside upper hoop, positioning so decoration hangs straight, and glue.

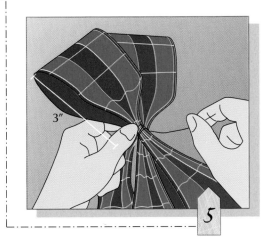

3"

Frosty & Rudolph
DOOR HANGERS

*F*rosty the Snowman and Rudolph the Red-Nosed Reindeer will jingle a hearty holiday welcome to all who walk through your doors. At 10" (25.5 cm) high, and using only half a sheet of plastic canvas, these stitch up very quickly, either for your own home, or to give as gifts to others.

MATERIALS

For Each Hanger
❋ 7-mesh plastic canvas, 1/2 sheet
❋ No. 16 tapestry needle
❋ 12 mm gold jingle bells, two

For Frosty
❋ Worsted-weight yarn: black, white, 10 yd. (9.15 m) each; red, 8 yd. (7.35 m); green, 3 yd. (2.75 m); bright pink, 1 yd. (0.95 m)

For Rudolph
❋ Worsted-weight yarn: medium brown, 15 yd. (13.8 m); tan, 12 yd. (11.04 m); green, 3 yd. (2.75 m); red, white, black, 1 yd. (0.95 m) each
❋ 3/4" (2 cm) red pom-pom
❋ Metallic green wire-edge ribbon: 1" (2.5 cm), 14" (35.5 cm); 1/4" (6 mm), 2" (5 cm)
❋ Hot glue gun
❋ Miscellaneous items: scissors, craft knife

1 Refer to the Plastic Canvas General Instructions and Stitches on page 156. Overcast all edges with matching yarn as you stitch.

2 **Rudolph:** Use long brown and red diagonal stitches for the ears and nose, and slanting green Gobelin stitches to work the collar. Fill in the eyes with black and white and the face with medium brown continental stitches. Highlight eyes with white French knots. Use black to backstitch mouth. Refer to the chart to tack a bell to tip of each ear. Hot-glue on pom-pom nose. Bend 1" (2.5 cm) ribbon into bow, and wrap narrow ribbon around center. Hot-glue bow to collar.

3 **Frosty:** Work hat and hatband in black and red slanting Gobelin stitches. Work green leaf stitches for holly leaves and a red cross-stitch for the berry. Work the red nose in padded satin stitch. Work continental stitches for the face, filling in unmarked areas with white. Use black to backstitch mouth and three scarf lines. Work the scarf with red and green continental and slanting Gobelin stitches. Use red yarn to tack bells to scarf.

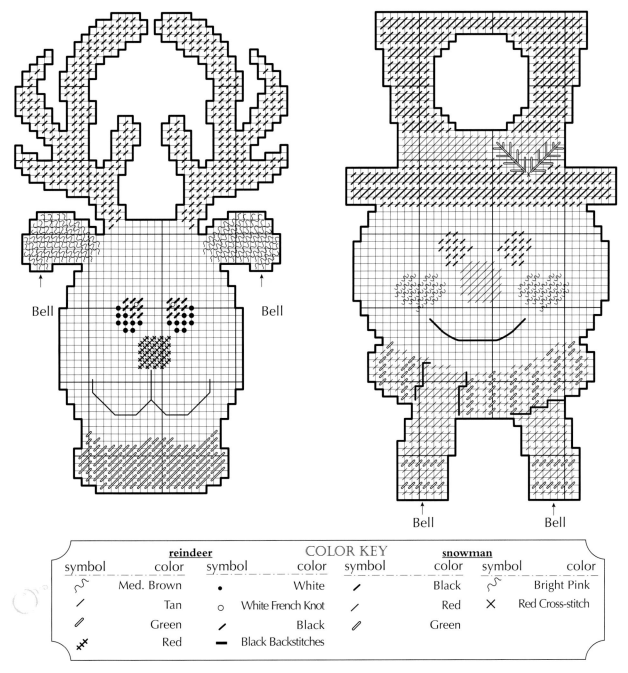

Bell Bell

Bell Bell

	reindeer	COLOR KEY			**snowman**		
symbol	color	symbol	color	symbol	color	symbol	color
∿	Med. Brown	•	White	╱	Black	∿	Bright Pink
╱	Tan	o	White French Knot	╱	Red	✕	Red Cross-stitch
╱	Green	╱	Black	╱	Green		
✕✕	Red	—	Black Backstitches				

HOLLY SLED

$\mathcal{W}$elcome your holiday visitors with this unique painted sled. It's perfect for hanging on a door or wall, or placing beside a fireplace—a sled you can enjoy whether or not there is snow on the ground! Painted with acrylics, the pretty holly and berry easy strokework design accents the Christmas message of NOEL. While our sled extends holiday greetings, you could also paint a family name in the center for a personal touch year-round.

MATERIALS
✳ Wood sled, 12" x 18" (30.5 x 46 cm)
✳ Tube acrylic paints: chrome oxide green, phthalo blue, burnt umber, bright red, alizarin crimson, titanium white, cadmium orange
✳ Paintbrushes: Nos. 10, 5, 3 round; No. 2 liner; 1" (2.5 cm) sponge, two
✳ ³/₈" (1 cm) red macramé cord, 1 yd. (0.95 m)
✳ Waterbase satin varnish for inside use or polyurethane varnish for outside use
✳ White craft glue
✳ Pattern sheet
✳ Miscellaneous items: fine sandpaper, waterbase wood sealer, soft paper towels, tracing paper, colored chalk, disposable palette, pencil

1. **Preparation:** Sand sled and apply one coat of wood sealer with sponge brush. Let dry and sand again lightly. Refer to page 158 for Painting Instructions and Techniques and to the photo for all steps below.

2. **Pattern:** Trace the four patterns onto tracing paper, reversing for left side slat and runner pieces. Draw over lines on back with chalk. Place chalk-side-down on sled and retrace lines on front to transfer. Pattern was designed for a 12" x 18" (30.5 x 46 cm) sled, but can easily be adapted to other sizes. See pattern for adjustments.

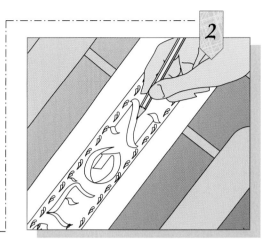

3. **Holly Leaves:** Mix phthalo blue with chrome oxide green for a blue-green shade. Paint holly leaves on right and left side slats using No. 10 brush and blue-green mixture. Shade a side of each leaf with a burnt umber line. With white, float highlight and add outline along edge of light side. Paint the veins with thinned burnt umber and highlight with white.

4. **Berries:** Paint with bright red. Mix a small amount of burnt umber with alizarin crimson and shade bottom of each berry. Highlight top of each berry with a mixture of cadmium orange and a touch of bright red. Add a white highlight to each berry.

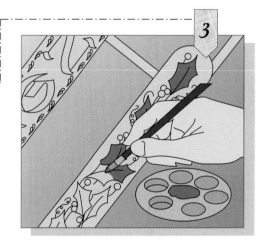

5. **Stems and Curlicues:** Use the liner brush and thinned burnt umber to paint the stems and curlicues on the right and left side slats.

6. **NOEL:** Paint the letters on the center slat using the No. 10 brush and blue-green mixture used for holly leaves. Use the No. 3 brush and blue-green mixture to paint small comma strokes all around edge of center slat.

7. **Runners and Crossbar:** Use the No. 5 brush and blue-green mixture to paint large comma strokes. Use the stylus or end of paintbrush handle to add red dots to runners, crossbar and center slat. Let dry.

8. **Finishing:** Apply varnish with sponge brush and let dry. Insert macramé cord ends through holes in crossbar, and knot on back. Add dot of glue to each knot.

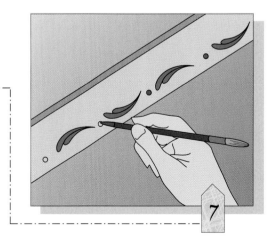

ELF CHILL CHASER

Sock it to Old Man Winter with this

cheerful Elf Chill Chaser made from

colorful recycled anklets, tights and ribbed

socks. His body, formed from a plastic bottle

and weighted with mini pellets, stays put on

a windowsill or under a door to keep out

those toe-tingling drafts and chills.

MATERIALS

* Red nylon tights, infant 12-18 mos.
* Socks:
white nylon anklet, misses size 9-11;
wide-ribbed cotton socks, girls size
7¹/₂-9: red, one; gray, one;
royal blue, two;
cotton anklets, infant 0-6 mos.: two
each; green, purple
* Yellow pom-poms: 1¹/₂" (3.8 cm),
one; 1" (2.5 cm), two
* 1-liter clear plastic bottle with
screw-on cap
* Polypropylene mini pellets,
2-pound (900 g) bag
* Polyester fiberfill
* Quilt batting, 16" x 31" (40.5 x
78.5 cm)
* 12 mm wiggle eyes, two
* Sewing threads: blue, white, purple
* Low-temp glue gun
* Miscellaneous items: sewing
needle, scissors, sewing machine

Legs: Lay quilt batting on flat surface. Pour approximately 6 oz. (170 g) of mini pellets down the center, lengthwise. Tightly roll the batting to form a 31" (78.5 cm) roll. Glue the seam and both ends closed. Cut roll into two 15½" (39.3 cm) rolls. Seal cut ends with glue. Insert one roll in each leg of the tights, leaving room in the center for the bottle.

1

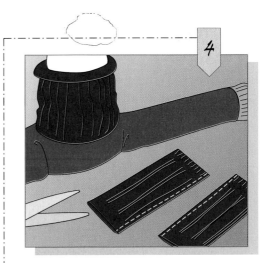

Body: Wash and dry plastic bottle. Fill with pellets and screw on cap. Place bottle into seat of tights and glue ends of batting rolls to sides of bottle. Insert extra fiberfill around bottom edge of bottle to fill out body. Pull white anklet over top of bottle.

2

Feet: Stuff toes of green socks. Pull a sock over each foot of tights. Fold down cuffs and spot-glue to tights. Glue a 1" (2.5 cm) pom-pom to each sock toe.

3

Sweater: Cut the ribbed cuffs off the blue socks, plus 1" (2.5 cm) of the sock foot. Pull the uncut edge of one cuff over the anklet-covered bottle. Roll down the upper cut edge to make a turtleneck collar. To make the sleeves, turn the second blue cuff inside out and sew two seams, ¼" (6 mm) apart, down the center. Cut between stitching lines, and turn each piece. Lightly stuff each sleeve and whipstitch the raw edges closed. Glue whipstitched side of sleeves to body at sides with sleeve tops even with sweater collar.

4

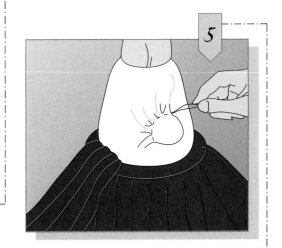

Face: Hand-baste a 1" (2.5 cm) circle on the front of the white anklet, ½" (1.3 cm) above the collar. Slit anklet at top of bottle. Insert stuffing through slit and behind circle; pull thread tight to form a puffball nose; knot. Glue wiggle eyes above nose.

5

Hat: Cut off cuff of red sock. Whipstitch raw edge closed. Pull over head and roll up bottom just above eyes in front; pull down to collar in back. Glue remaining yellow pom-pom to top of hat. Spot-glue hat to head.

6

Mittens: See the illustration to tack thumbs in purple socks. Use matching thread, insert needle at dot. Whipstitch around sole so that sock heel forms mitten thumb. Pull thread tight, and knot. Roll cuffs down, stuff with fiberfill and spot-glue to bottom of sleeves.

7

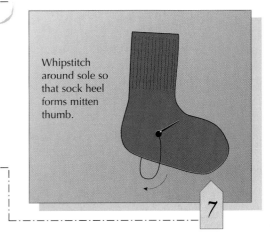

Whipstitch around sole so that sock heel forms mitten thumb.

Scarf: Turn gray sock inside out. Sew two seams ¼" (6 mm) apart, down center of sock. Cut between seamlines; turn. Overlap and glue the toe ends together. Tie scarf around neck.

8

RUSTIC SANTA

$\mathcal{H}$e's a merry fellow, this rustic wooden Santa. He'll dance from your door whenever you open it to greet Christmas guests and friends. His body, arms and legs are cut from wood, then painted and sanded for a weathered, antique look. Add hand-carved details and a bit o' wire for a wonderful Santa who'll "hang around" for years to come.

MATERIALS

❋ 1" (2.5 cm) pine wood, 10" x 18" (25.5 x 46 cm)

❋ Acrylic paints: huckleberry red, rose, gold, black, green, peach, antique white

❋ Dark oak wood stain

❋ Paintbrushes: fine liner, No. 10 flat, small stencil, 1" (2.5 cm) sponge

❋ 18-gauge black spool wire

❋ Band or jig saw with ¹/₈" (3 mm) blade

❋ Drill with ¹/₁₆" bit

❋ Pattern sheet

❋ Miscellaneous items: tracing paper, pencil, graphite paper, stylus, ruler, fine sandpaper, tack cloth, craft or utility knife with extra blades, masking tape, soft clean cloth, mineral spirits or turpentine, wire cutters, needlenose pliers

1 Trace the six patterns onto tracing paper, and use graphite paper and stylus to transfer outlines only to wood. Cut from wood using band saw. Sand all pieces to smooth rough edges, and wipe with tack cloth. Lightly transfer detail lines with graphite paper and stylus.

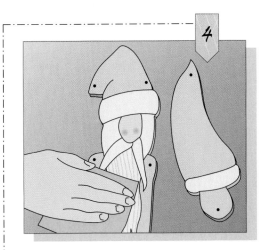

2 **Painting:** Refer to page 158 for Painting Instructions and Techniques. Thin all paints to an ink-like consistency. Extend painting over edges where possible. Outline all sections with liner brush, then fill in with No. 10 flat brush.

3 Paint Santa's face with peach. Let dry. Cover mustache and hair with masking tape. Apply rose to cheeks with stencil brush. Let dry, and remove tape. Paint hair, mustache and beard, and fur on hat, sleeves, coat and pants with antique white. Let dry.

4 Lightly sand painted areas in the direction of the wood grain, until wood shows through in random spots. Wipe with tack cloth.

5 Paint boots and mittens with thinned black. Dip brush handle tip in black and dot Santa's eyes, slightly off-center to give him a whimsical look. Paint jacket, pants, sleeves and hat with huckleberry red. Paint star gold and tree green. Let dry. Repeat Step 4 for remaining painted surfaces.

6 **Carving:** Practice cutting a small groove with craft or utility knife on a piece of scrap wood. Use a sharp blade and change blades often to make clean and neat cuts. Shave edges of all pieces with knife to give a weathered rustic look. Sand all cut edges, and wipe with tack cloth. Score, then cut inward on each side of lines to carve a small V-shaped groove along beard, mustache, face and all fur outlines. Score, do <u>not</u> cut, the detail lines in beard, mustache, hair and fur.

7 **Antiquing:** Brush stain on each piece with sponge brush, and wipe off excess, as desired, with soft cloth. Let dry.

8 **Assembly:** Drill holes as marked on patterns. Cut wire into six 4" (10 cm), two 9" (23 cm), and two 18" (46 cm) lengths. Use 4" (10 cm) wires to wire lower pants to upper pants, upper pants to body, and arms to shoulders, inserting wire front to back. Leave space between pieces for movement. Twist ends with pliers and tuck between pieces.

9 Wrap one end of a 9" (23 cm) wire three times around a pencil to curl. Insert straight end through star front, then through the back of the right mitten to front; curl end. Repeat to attach tree to left mitten.

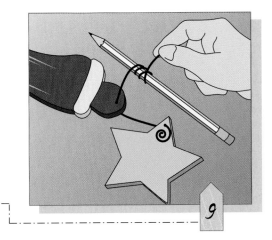

10 Twist ends of 18" (46 cm) wires around each other several times. Insert ends, front to back, through hat holes for hanger. Twist ends to secure.

WALL TREE

ake a stunning

wall accent from a

miniature artificial pine tree

by bending the branches to the

front, which creates a flat surface in the

back. This allows the tree to be displayed

flat against a wall. The wall tree is then

embellished with a variety of fruit and is

topped with a large bow.

MATERIALS
❋ Artificial pine tree with attached trunk, about 24" (61 cm) tall
❋ Four or five varieties of fruit, including apples,
pears, grape clusters, and berries
❋ Metallic gold aerosol spray paint
❋ Preserved leaves on stems
❋ 3 yd. (2.75 m) wired ribbon, for bow
❋ Floral wire
❋ Miscellaneous items: hot glue gun, glue sticks, scissors, plastic

1 Bend branches of artificial tree around to one side. Place flat on table, and arrange branches.

2 Hot glue pears to tree, forming a curved diagonal line as shown.

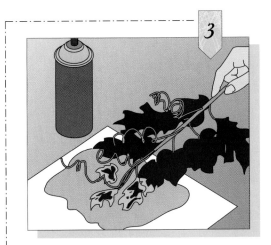

3 Place a sheet of plastic on work surface. Spray a generous pool of gold aerosol paint onto plastic. Drag preserved leaves through the paint to gild them. Allow to dry. Repeat with additional colors, if desired. —·—·—·—·—

4 Hot-glue a thin layer of gilded leaves along sides of pears. Lift pine boughs to surround the row of pears and leaves. Insert second variety of fruit and another row of gilded leaves, following the same line as the pears; secure with hot glue. —·—·—·—·—

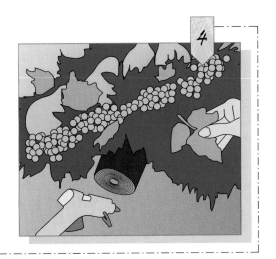

5 Continue to hot-glue alternating rows of fruit and gilded leaves, until the entire tree is covered. Arrange pine boughs between rows of fruit and leaves.

6 Form large loops from wired ribbon as shown. Continue to make six loops. Make small loop at center. Bend wire around ribbon at center; twist wire tightly, gathering ribbon. Separate and shape the loops. —·—·—·—·—

7 Wire bow to top of tree. Twist excess wire into loop at back, for hanging tree. Tuck ends of ribbon into sides of tree.

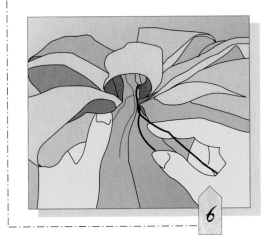

stars & candles
WALL QUILT

$\mathcal{P}$recut iron-on adhesive tape saves time and effort in fusing the geometric shapes cut from ribbons and bright-colored fabrics. You'll have fun creating this mock quilt symbolizing the magic of candlelight and stars—a fitting theme for a holiday wall hanging.

MATERIALS

❋ 45″ (115 cm) cotton fabrics: tone-on-tone white, 3/4 yd. (0.7 m); Christmas print for backing, 3/4 yd. (0.7 m); solids, 1/8 yd. (0.15 m) each: red, green, gold, royal blue
❋ Red ribbon: 1 3/8″ (3.5 cm) plaid taffeta, 2 2/3 yd. (2.48 m); 3/8″ satin (1 cm), 5 1/4 yd. (4.8 m); 7/8″ (2.2 cm) satin, 3 yd. (2.75 m)
❋ Fusible web, 1/2 yd. (0.5 m)
❋ Iron-on adhesive tape: 3/8″ (1 cm), 7/8″ (2.2 cm); one package each
❋ Craft fleece, 27″ (68.5 cm) square
❋ Rotary cutter and mat
❋ Transparent ruler with 45° angle and 5/8″ (1.5 cm) marking
❋ Pattern sheet
❋ Miscellaneous items: scissors, ruler, yardstick, pencil, straight pins, iron

1 **Preparation:** Prewash and press all fabrics. Cut one 27" (68.5 cm) white tone-on-tone fabric square for quilt front and one 27" (68.5 cm) square of Christmas print for backing.

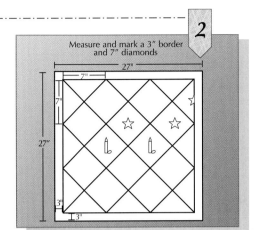

Measure and mark a 3" border and 7" diamonds

2 See the illustration to lightly pencil-mark border and diamonds on the tone-on-tone quilt front.

3 **Stars and Candles:** Follow manufacturer's instructions to fuse a 4" x 17" (10 x 43 cm) piece of fusible web to the back of the four solid-color fabrics. From each, rotary-cut two ⅝" x 17" (1.5 x 43 cm) strips and one 1⅜" (3.5 cm) square. Remove backing paper.

4 Cut two ⅝" x 3" (1.5 x 7.5 cm) strips from red, blue and green for the candles. Then use the 45° angle on the ruler to cut fused fabric strips at every ⅝" (1.5 cm) mark to make 24 diamond shapes of each color.

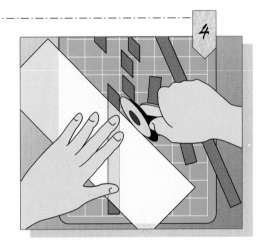

5 Trace the candle flame and candle holder patterns and cut six of each from fused gold fabric.

6 **Diagonal Red Ribbon Strips:** From both ⅜" (1 cm) adhesive tape and the ⅜" (1 cm) red satin ribbon, cut the following lengths: 30" (76 cm), two; 21" (53.5 cm), four; and 11" (28 cm), four. Fuse tape to wrong side of the ribbon.

7 **Binding:** Cut four 27" (68.5 cm) lengths each of the ⅞" (2.2 cm) red satin ribbon and adhesive tape.

8 **Border:** Cut four 22" (56 cm) lengths of the 1⅜" (3.5 cm) plaid ribbon and eight 21" (53.5 cm) lengths of ⅜" (1 cm) adhesive tape. Ribbon may shrink when fusing; trim to 21"(53.5 cm). Fuse two ⅜" (1 cm) tape strips to back edges of each plaid ribbon length.

9 **Assembly:** Center and fuse the ⅜" (1 cm) red satin ribbon strips over the diagonal pencil lines on quilt front. Fuse plaid ribbon strips along penciled border. Fuse one fabric square on each plaid corner.

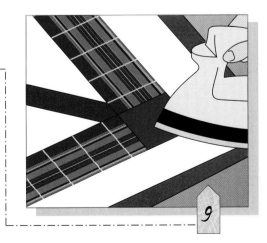

10 Refer to the photo to position and fuse the candles and stars in center of alternating diamonds. Arrange stars in same color sequence. Fuse half stars to center of half squares along plaid ribbon border.

11 Sandwich and pin the fleece between quilt top and backing. Fold the fused ⅞" (2.2 cm) red satin ribbon in half lengthwise, and fuse around outer front edge. Repeat to fuse other half on back.

quick-tuck
QUILT WREATH

If you think you need a needle, thread and batting to quilt, think again! Use a pencil to score quilt block patterns onto foam squares, then cover them with fabric, tucking the pieces into the scored lines with a putty knife. It's that easy! Once you've tried it yourself, host a Christmas "quilting bee" with a few friends to make a handsome holiday wreath.

MATERIALS

❋ 24" (61 cm) artificial pine wreath

❋ Styrofoam®: 1/2" x 12" x 36" (1.3 x 30.5 x 91.5 cm) sheet, one; 1" (2.5 cm) balls, 12

❋ 45" (115 cm) cotton fabrics: 1/4 yd. (0.25 m) muslin; 3/8 yd. (0.35 m) off-white Christmas print; 1/8 yd. (0.15 m) each: dark green solid, dark green plaid, red minicheck and red miniprint

❋ Dark green ribbon: 3/8" (1 cm) grosgrain, 21/2 yd. (2.3 m); 1/8" (3 mm) satin, 1/2 yd. (0.5 m)

❋ Buttons: 1/4" to 3/8" (6 mm to 1 cm) assorted flat, 15; 1/2" (1.3 cm) gold novelty thimble, six

❋ 1 oz. (30 g) natural gypsophila

❋ Cloth-covered floral wire, 18" (46 cm) lengths, seven

❋ Green chenille stem, one

❋ Fabric stiffener

❋ Glues: low-temp glue gun, thick white craft glue

❋ Battery-operated minilight strings

❋ Pattern sheet

❋ Miscellaneous items: tracing paper, pencil, scissors, wire cutters, cutting board, serrated steak knife, putty knife, paraffin or candle stub, straight pins, sealable quart-size plastic bag, measuring cup, wax paper, paper towels, rotary cutter and mat (optional)

1 **Cutting Foam:** Wax the serrated knife blade, then use a sawing motion to cut squares from the foam sheet as follows: two 4" (10 cm), three 3" (7.5 cm), and seven 1" (2.5 cm). To smooth the rough edges, rub with a scrap piece of foam.

2 **Quilt Blocks:** Trace the five block patterns, including the letters. Cut out block outlines and pin to foam squares. Trace over pattern lines with a sharp pencil to score the foam; remove the patterns.

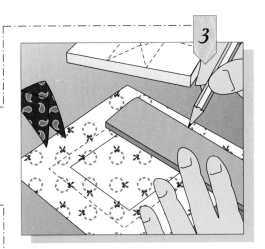

3 Cut paper patterns apart along pattern lines. Cut out the fabric pieces following Color Key. From muslin, cut two 4½" (11.5 cm), three 3½" (9 cm) and seven 1½" (3.8 cm) squares for the ornament backings. See illustration to **add ¼" (6 mm) seam allowance on all sides.** ─ ─ ─ ─ ─ ─ ─ ─ ─ ─

4 Place the middle fabric piece, right side up, over center area on foam square. See illustration for how to use the putty knife to tuck the fabric edges into the scored lines. Clip the excess fabric, being careful not to cut the tucked fabric. Repeat to tuck the remaining fabric pieces, working out from the center. Fold and glue the excess fabric to the foam edges. ─ ─ ─ ─

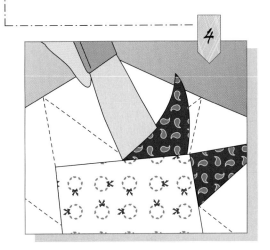

5 Center and pin a muslin square to ornament backs, then fold and glue the excess fabric to the foam edges; remove pins. Starting at a corner, glue the green grosgrain ribbon to cover the foam square edges, overlapping ends ½" (1.3 cm).

6 **Block C:** Glue a cluster of six flat buttons to the center top of the basket. Cut two 6" (15 cm) satin ribbons and tie one in a small bow. Glue the ends of the remaining ribbon to the top of the basket ½" (1.3 cm) from the sides for a handle. Glue the bow to the top of the handle.

7 **Block A:** Glue nine flat buttons randomly to the plaid wreath. Tie the remaining 6" (15 cm) satin ribbon in a bow and glue to the wreath.

8 **1" (2.5 cm) Blocks:** Cut the following 1½" (3.8 cm) fabric squares: red minicheck, dark green plaid, two each; and red miniprint, three. Center each print fabric square on a foam square, then fold and glue the excess fabric to the edges. Repeat to cover the backs with muslin. Refer to Step 5 to glue ribbon to cover edges.

9 **Balls:** Cut three ¼" x 45" (6 mm x 115 cm) fabric strips from muslin and dark green plaid; and from red minicheck, six. Wrap a strip around each ball to cover; spot-glue end.

10 **Bow:** Tear three 1¾" x 45" (4.5 x 115 cm) strips from the off-white Christmas print fabric. Pour ¼ cup (59 mL) each of fabric stiffener and water into the plastic bag, then place the fabric strips inside the bag as shown. Standing over a sink, remove saturated strips and squeeze out the excess liquid. Place the strips on wax paper and blot with paper towels; line dry. Make an 8-loop bow with streamers. Secure it with wire and attach it to the center bottom of the wreath. ─ ─ ─ ─ ─ ─ ─ ─

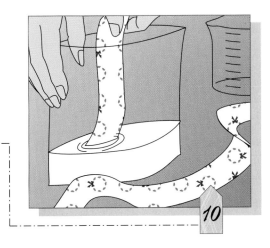

11 **Assembly:** Refer to the photo to hot-glue quilt block ornaments to the wreath. Fill in with fabric-covered squares and balls. Glue small clusters of gypsophila around the wreath. Use 3" (7.5 cm) lengths of wire to attach the thimble buttons to the wreath. Attach the chenille stem to the top center back of the wreath; twist ends together to form a loop hanger. If desired, wrap the lights around the wreath, hiding the battery packs in the back.

QUILTED NATIVITY

The traditional nativity is interpreted here in a 20" x 20" (51 x 51 cm) quilted nativity wall hanging which features appliqué and embroidery details. Cotton fabrics in rustic browns and shades of purple are pieced in log-cabin-like blocks to form the background and garments for Mary and Joseph. Appliquéd faces and the shining star complete this handsome quilt to hang from door, wall, or above a fireplace.

MATERIALS

* 45" (115 cm) cotton solid fabrics: dark lavender, 1/4 yd. (0.25 m); peach and cream, 1/8 yd. (0.15 m) each
* 45" (115 cm) cotton print fabrics: brown, 1/4 yd. (0.25 m); two coordinating light blue and purple prints, 1/3 yd. (0.32 m) each; purple pin-dot for backing, 2/3 yd. (0.63 m); gold, 1/8 yd. (0.15 m)
* 22" (56 cm) square low-loft batting
* 1" (2.5 cm) bias tape, dark brown, one package

* Embroidery floss: gold, brown
* Pink fabric crayon
* Rotary cutter and mat
* Needles: Size 10 quilting, embroidery
* Quilting thread
* Pattern sheet
* Miscellaneous items: matching threads, scissors, sewing machine, straight pins, tape measure, sewing needle, tracing paper, pencil, iron, plastic or cardboard for template, masking tape

1   **Patterns and Cutting:** Prewash and press all fabrics. Unless otherwise indicated, sew pieces right sides together using a ¼" (6 mm) seam allowance. Use the rotary cutter and mat to cut fabrics and trim strips where necessary.

2   Trace the ten patterns and cut from fabrics as directed. Trace the embroidery details onto face, hands and blanket pieces. Cut two 3" (7.5 cm) light blue strips for the border, and the remaining gold, light blue, brown, purple and dark lavender fabric into 1" (2.5 cm) strips. Do not cut purple pin-dot backing fabric yet.

3   **Piecing:** It is important to cut and stitch accurately, so the pieces will fit together exactly with matching corners. Use a stitch length of 15 stitches per inch (centimeter). Match thread color to darkest fabrics, or use a neutral color such as black or gray. Press seams to one side, rather than open, and to the darker fabric to prevent show-through. Use steam, rather than pressure, to prevent imprinting. Press blocks first from wrong side, then from right side. A quilt should not be pressed after completion; pressing will flatten the batting.

4   **Courthouse Steps Blocks:** Begin with a solid purple block and follow the Step 4 illustration. Cut a 1" (2.5 cm) square from strip, place on purple strip as shown in A, and stitch. Cut even with square; press open as in B.

5   Place the pieced unit on purple strip as shown in C, and stitch. Cut even with pieced unit; press open as in D. Place pieced unit on purple strip as shown in E, and stitch. Cut even with pieced unit; press open as in F.

6   Repeat the stitching, cutting even, and pressing steps to stitch all 13 pieces in numerical order to make one purple Courthouse Steps Block. Follow the Color Piecing Guide on next page to make the 13 Courthouse Steps blocks in the colors shown.

7   **Log Cabin Blocks:** Begin with purple/brown block shown in Color Piecing Guide, and follow the Step 7 illustration. Cut a 1" (2.5 cm) purple square and place on a brown strip as shown in A, and stitch. Cut even with square; press open as in B.

8   Place brown strip at a 90° angle to previous piece as shown in C, and stitch. Cut strip even with pieced unit, and press as shown in D. Place purple strip at a 90° angle to previous piece as shown in E, and stitch. Cut strip even with pieced unit, and press as shown in F.

9   Repeat the stitching, cutting even, and pressing steps to stitch all 13 pieces in numerical order to make one Log Cabin Block. Follow the Color Piecing Guide on next page to make the 12 Log Cabin blocks in color combinations shown.

10   **Assembly:** Refer to the Assembly Guide on the next page to stitch the blocks together in 5-block rows. Stitch the rows together to complete the nativity scene blocked unit; press.

11   **Sashing Strips:** Stitch a 1" (2.5 cm) gold strip to the bottom, and 1" (2.5) brown strips to the sides and top. Cut strips even, and press.

12   **Borders:** Measure quilt top across the middle. Use the 3" (7.5 cm) strips and cut 2 pieces with the length equal to middle measurement plus 6½" (16.3 cm). Repeat for side borders, measuring quilt down the middle from top to bottom.

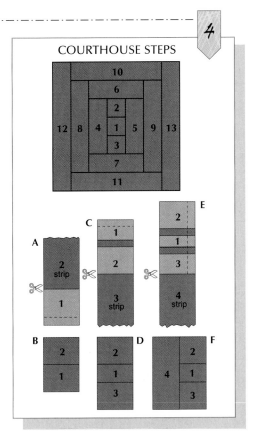

COURTHOUSE STEPS

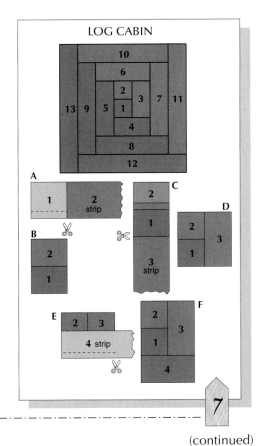

LOG CABIN

(continued)

13 Pin-mark center of quilt top along top and bottom edges. Pin-mark centers of top and bottom border strips. Pin-mark 3¼" (8.2 cm) in from each end of border strips. Place border strip on quilt top, right sides together. Match pin marks at center and pin marks at end of borders to quilt top edges. Pin border to quilt top, easing in any fullness. Stitch, beginning and ending ¼" (6 mm) in from edges; backstitch at ends. Repeat Step 13 for quilt top sides.

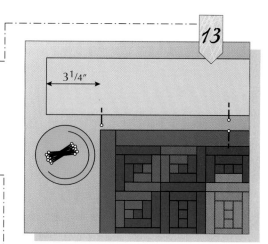

14 Fold quilt top at corner diagonally, right sides together. Match border seamlines; pin securely. Draw a diagonal line on border strip, extending line formed by quilt top fold. Stitch on the line; do not catch the seam allowances in the stitching. Trim ends of border strips to ¼" (6 mm) seam allowances. Press mitered seam allowances open at border; press remaining seam allowances toward border strip. Repeat for remaining corners.

15 **Appliquéing:** Press the seam allowance under on appliqué pieces; clip outward curves and inward corners as necessary. Refer to the Appliqué Guide to position each piece. Either hand-appliqué or machine-blindstitch or satin stitch. The quilt in this photo was hand-appliquéd. Appliqué the straw, blanket, faces, hands, Joseph's beard and staff. Piece the star, then appliqué at upper right.

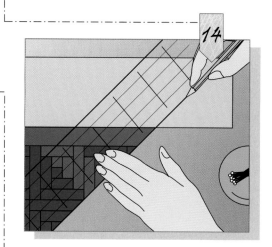

16 **Embroidering:** See patterns for stitching lines, and use the outline stitch in the illustration to embroider details. Use one strand of brown floss for the facial features, Baby's hair, Joseph's beard, hair and hands, and Mary's hair. Use two strands of gold for the Baby's halo and blanket cord.

17 **Marking:** Cut a template from border quilting template pattern. Center and mark the quilting lines on borders, reversing pattern for opposite side.

18 **Basting:** Cut batting and purple pindot fabric so 2" to 4" (5 to 10 cm) extends beyond quilt top on each side. Pin-mark the center of each side for quilt top, backing and batting.

19 Tape backing, wrong side up, to hard, flat work surface. Begin at center, and work toward corners, stretching fabric slightly. Place batting over backing, matching at centers. Smooth, but do not stretch, working from center outward. Repeat for quilt top.

20 Pin-baste a line up the middle of each side, starting at center. Baste each quarter, placing pins in rows about 5" (12.5 cm) apart. Avoid basting on quilting lines. Remove tape from backing; fold backing edges over batting and quilt top to prevent raveling, and pin.

21 **Quilting:** Hand-quilt along marked border design lines and around the star, Mary, Joseph, Baby, manger, and stable.

22 **Finishing:** Carefully round off border corners to a soft curve, using a plate or bowl as a guide, and bind with bias tape. Cut a muslin sleeve for hanging 10" (25.5 cm) wide by the width of the quilt. Turn under and stitch ½" (1.3 cm) double-fold hems on short ends. Stitch long edges in ½" (1.3 cm) seam, right sides together. Turn right side out; press flat, centering seam. Pin sleeve at top on back, hand-stitch all around, only going through batting and backing layers. Hang on a dowel or wooden piece.

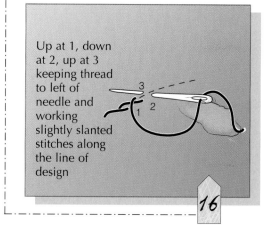

Up at 1, down at 2, up at 3 keeping thread to left of needle and working slightly slanted stitches along the line of design

COLOR PIECING GUIDE

Courthouse Steps

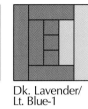

Purple-7

Dk. Lavender-2

Lt. Blue-1

Dk. Lavender/ Lt. Blue-1

Brown-1

Purple/Dk. Lavender-1

Log Cabin

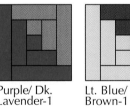

Purple/ Brown-6

Lt. Blue/ Purple-2

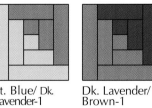

Purple/ Dk. Lavender-1

Lt. Blue/ Brown-1

Lt. Blue/ Dk. Lavender-1

Dk. Lavender/ Brown-1

COLOR KEY
- Lt. Blue
- Dk. Lavender
- Purple
- Brown

ASSEMBLY GUIDE

COLOR KEY
- Lt. Blue
- Dk. Lavender
- Purple
- Brown
- Gold

APPLIQUÉ GUIDE

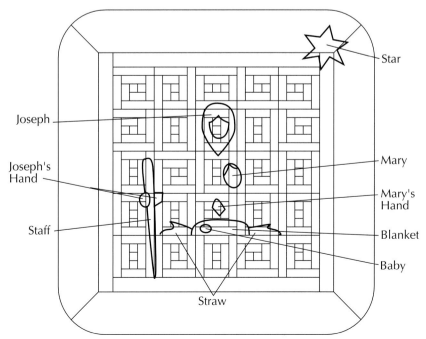

Star

Joseph

Mary

Joseph's Hand

Mary's Hand

Staff

Blanket

Baby

Straw

RIBBON SWAG

$\mathcal{P}$eek beneath the richly colored cranberry and hunter green satin loops and you'll find... a yardstick! While you're hanging the stockings with care, take a few moments to craft this attractive swag. Displayed above the fireplace mantel or over a doorway, your Christmas decor is sure to "measure" up!

MATERIALS
❋ Yardstick
❋ 2″ (5 cm) wide satin ribbon: hunter green, cranberry; 3 yd. (2.75 m) each
❋ 1¹⁄₂″ (3.8 cm) to 2″ (5 cm) wired pinecones, 16
❋ Metallic gold spray paint
❋ German statice sprigs, 10
❋ 24-gauge wire
❋ Low-temp glue gun
❋ Miscellaneous items: scissors, ruler, wire cutters, spray bottle with water

1 Follow manufacturer's instructions to spray the pinecones with metallic gold paint.

2 Cut the following ribbon lengths: hunter green, six 12" (30.5 cm), one 36" (91.5 cm); cranberry, five 12" (30.5 cm), one 38" (96.5 cm), and one 8" (20.5 cm).

3 Untwist all satin ribbon pieces. Open one end and run thumb down center. To relax folds, lightly mist wrong side with water and gently spread. Let dry.

4 Bring cut ends of each 12" (30.5 cm) ribbon length together. Wrap wire around ends to make eleven loops.

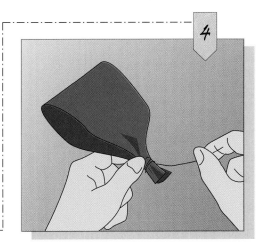

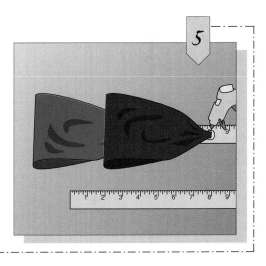

5 Refer to the photo and begin at outer edge, working toward center. Hot-glue wired base of alternating color loops along yardstick at the following inch marks: 4" (10 cm), 8" (20.5 cm), 12" (30.5 cm), 15" (38 cm); repeat at opposite end at 32" (81.5 cm), 28" (71 cm), and 24" (61 cm), and 21" (53.5 cm).

6 Glue base of the remaining cranberry loop vertically to yardstick at 18" (46 cm) mark. Angle and glue one green loop to each side of cranberry loop.

7 See the illustration to wire a bow using the 36" (91.5 cm) green ribbon. Gather ribbon at center, shown by dotted line, and wrap with wire, forming 5½" (14 cm) loops on each side of center. Repeat to wire a cranberry bow using 38" (96.5 cm) ribbon and forming 4½" (11.5 cm) loops on each side. Form a loop with remaining cranberry ribbon and wire to center of bow. Center cranberry bow on top of green bow, and wire to yardstick center. Cut inverted V's in ribbon ends.

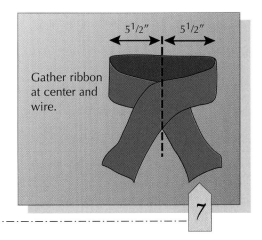

Gather ribbon at center and wire.

5½"   5½"

8 To decorate, refer to the photo to glue pinecones to each side of green bow. Glue statice sprigs between loops.

MENORAH

paper-twist

Paper crafting adds a new twist to the traditional Jewish celebration of the Festival of Lights. During Chanukah, the eight-day Jewish holiday, families light a candle on the first night and an additional candle on each succeeding night. The traditional candle holder, the menorah, is symbolic with its eight branches and a ninth branch for the leader candle, or "Shammesh," which always remains lit and is used to light the other candles.

MATERIALS
* Stiff cardboard, 9" x 16" (23 x 40.5 cm)
* Paper twist: blue, 2 yd. (1.85 m); white, 1 yd. (0.95 m)
* Gold metallic tinsel stems, 12
* Miscellaneous items: scissors, craft glue, ruler, craft knife (optional)

1 **Cardboard Base:** Refer to the illustration to mark and cut 1¼" (3.2 cm) wide strips from stiff cardboard.

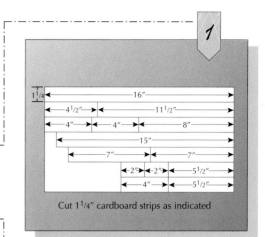

Cut 1¼" cardboard strips as indicated

2 Refer to the illustration to assemble the center stem and four individual branches. Use scissors to round corners where indicated. Glue strips together at intersection points.

3 **Wrapping:** Spiral-wrap the center stem and No. 2 and 4 branches with blue paper twist and No. 1 and 3 branches with white paper twist. Spot-glue where needed; fold ends to back, and glue.

4 **Assembly:** Measure 9" (23 cm) from top front of center stem and position branch No. 1 at this point. Refer to the photo to weave No. 2 branch over No. 1 branch and behind center stem. Repeat to weave No. 3 and 4 branches over and under center stem and branches. Adjust tops of branches to even them out.

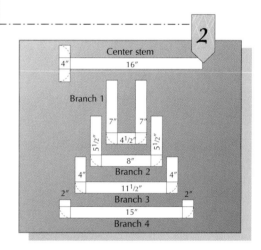

Center stem

Branch 1

Branch 2

Branch 3

Branch 4

5 Refer to the photo to wrap each Branch 4 intersection with gold tinsel stem, to make an X. Twist at back to secure. Twist a gold loop at the back of the center branch for hanging.

6 **Candle Flames:** Fold tinsel stem in half. Pinch a 1½" (3.8 cm) loop in center and another smaller loop inside first loop, twisting end around center of stem. Repeat to make nine flames.

7 See illustration to attach each flame to center stem, and wrap tinsel stem around front of stem ½" (1.3 cm) from top with flame extending above stem. Twist tightly at back.

8 **Storage:** To take apart and store, unwind tinsel stems and separate branches.

TIN-PUNCH SANTA

Crafting is as much a part of the holidays as Christmas baking, so combine the two by punching a design on the bottom of a pie pan. Paint St. Nick to bring him to life, and add a decorative paper-twist bow and silk holly leaves. This cute pie-pan wreath will not only satisfy your crafting sweet tooth, but will also make a quick-and-easy hostess gift.

MATERIALS

* 9" (23 cm) metal pie pan
* Tools: hammer, awl
* Acrylic paints: red, dark green, peach, ivory, black
* Antiquing stain
* Paintbrushes: small flat, 1" (2.5 cm) sponge
* Clear matte acrylic spray
* Red paper twist, 1½ yd. (1.4 m)
* Silk holly pick
* Fine-gauge wire, 6" (15 cm)
* Jute, 5" (12.5 cm)
* Hot glue gun
* Pattern sheet
* Miscellaneous items: pencil, scissors, wire cutters, tracing paper, masking tape, soft cloth; paper towels, newspapers

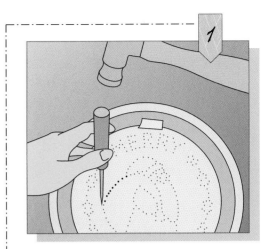

1   Trace the pattern and cut out the circle. Tape pattern to pie-pan bottom as shown in illustration. Use the hammer and awl to punch design holes through pan. — - -

    2   Use the sponge brush to antique outside of pan. Wipe excess with soft cloth; let dry. Seal with acrylic spray.

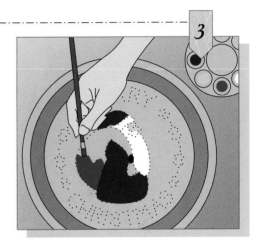

3   Use the small flat brush to paint the following with two coats of paint: Santa suit and hat with red, face with peach, beard, mustache and fur trim with ivory, mitten with black and bag with green. Let dry. Seal with two coats of acrylic spray. — - -

    4   Cut a paper-twist length to fit pan rim. See illustration to hot-glue to pan, overlapping ends at the top. Untwist remaining paper twist, and wire a two-loop bow with short tails. Hot-glue bow to rim at center top. — - -

5   Remove holly leaves and berries from pick. Refer to the photo to hot-glue holly leaves to front of bow, and berries to bow center. Glue jute ends to inside rim at center top for loop hanger.

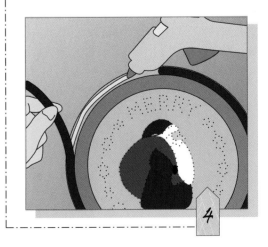

HOLIDAY WREATH & CENTERPIECE

Sparkling silver mesh ribbon and berries are a striking contrast to the burgundy rosebuds nestled among pinecones and evergreen sprays which accent this Christmas combo for your home. Greeting your guests at the door with a wreath, then finding a matching centerpiece at the table will set a festive mood for an evening dinner party.

MATERIALS

For the Wreath
* 11" (28 cm) willow wreath
* Silver spray paint
* Artificial pine sprays, 11" (28 cm), four
* Burgundy rosebuds, five
* Pink phlox floral stems, five
* Pinecones, 3" (7.5 cm) slender, two
* Silver wired balls: 12 mm, 15 mm; eight each
* 3" (7.5 cm) silver mesh ribbon, 1 yd. (0.95 m)

For Both
* Green floral tape
* 24-gauge green wire
* Miscellaneous Items: scissors, ruler, wire cutters, hot glue gun

For the Centerpiece
* 6" (15 cm) round flat silver floral container
* 6" x 2" (15 x 5 cm) Stryofoam® disc
* Artificial pine sprays, 11" (28 cm), eight
* Pinecones, 4 1/2" (11.5 cm) slender, six
* 7" (18 cm) pink candle and candle holder
* 3" (7.5 cm) silver mesh ribbon, 1 1/2 yd. (1.4 m)
* Burgundy rosebuds with leaves, eight
* Pink phlox floral stems, 12
* 23 mm wired silver balls, 10

1 **Wreath:** Spray paint wreath silver; let dry. Refer to the photo for all steps below.

2 See the illustration to wire pine sprays as follows: Wire No. 1 and 2 pine sprays together to measure 14" (35.5 cm) tip to tip. Wire No. 3 and 4 sprays to fill in between Nos. 1 and 2. Center the pine sprays vertically onto wreath and wire in place.

3 Cut four 8" (20.5 cm) silver mesh ribbon lengths, and wire each into a loop. Hot-glue the loops diagonally into pine sprays.

4 Hot-glue the pinecones diagonally, one on each side of center. Wrap floral tape around a phlox stem and a rosebud stem, making five clusters. Randomly glue clusters to pine sprays. Glue clusters of silver balls randomly between pine sprays.

5 **Centerpiece:** Hot-glue foam disc inside container, applying glue to container, rather than foam. Insert candle holder and candle in center of foam.

6 See the illustration to insert and hot-glue pine sprays into foam disc as follows: Insert Nos. 1 and 2 to measure 20" (51 cm) tip to tip, Nos. 3 and 4 to measure 14" (35.5 cm) and Nos. 5 to 8 diagonally between.

7 Cut six 8" (20.5 cm) silver mesh ribbon lengths, and wire each into a loop. Center and hot-glue three loops on either side of candle holder in a straight line. Cut one 5" (12.5 cm) ribbon length. Wrap and glue around center of candle. Glue three clusters of phlox to cover ribbon seam.

8 Randomly glue pinecones between pine sprays. Tape two clusters, each with two phlox sprigs and one rosebud. Glue one to front and back of candle base. With remaining flowers, make clusters of one rosebud and phlox sprigs. Randomly glue clusters and silver balls onto pine sprays.

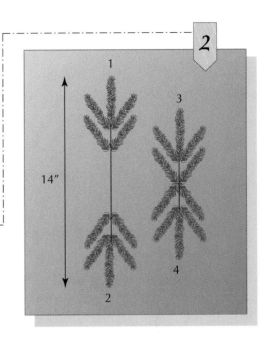

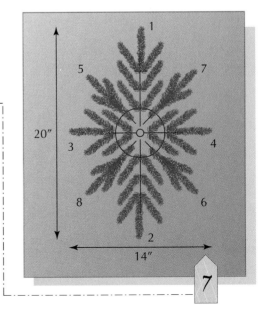

HOLLY-DAYS TABLE RUNNER

'Tis the season to be entertaining, so make a stunning table runner for limitless use throughout the Yuletide season! Along with the Christmas goose, this runner will be a main attraction at your holiday dinner table. Cut artist canvas to your desired size, then sponge paint with two rich colors of teal green. Stencil holly vining around a gold border; then it's ready to varnish and use—over and over again by simply wiping clean.

MATERIALS

* 53" (134.5 cm) primed artist canvas (available at art supply stores), 1/2 yd. (0.5 m)
* Stencil plastic
* Acrylic paints: light teal green, dark teal green and gold; metallics: gold, green and red
* Matte waterbase varnish
* Paintbrushes: No. 1 script, 1" (2.5 cm) foam
* Small natural sea sponges, three
* Black fine-point marker
* Pattern sheet
* Miscellaneous items: scissors, ruler, yardstick, palette, brush basin, paper towels, scrap paper, white chalk, pencil, masking tape, credit card, craft knife with No. 11 blade, cutting surface, newspapers, transparent quilting ruler (optional), hole punch (optional)

Preparation: Cut canvas to measure 14½" x 53" (36.8 x 134.5 cm) or desired size for table runner. Use the foam brush to basecoat entire table runner light teal green; let dry. Refer to photo for all steps below.

1

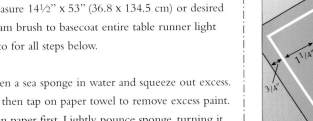
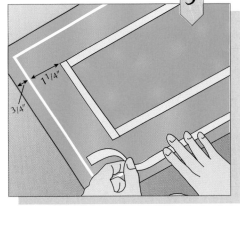

Sponge Painting: Dampen a sea sponge in water and squeeze out excess. Dip sponge into dark teal, then tap on paper towel to remove excess paint. Practice sponge painting on paper first. Lightly pounce sponge, turning it in different directions and tapping it randomly to avoid rows of color. If too much color is applied or rows appear, sponge lightly with light teal to lighten. Let dry thoroughly.

2

Border: Measure and mark with white chalk a 1¼" (3.2 cm) wide border ¾" (2 cm) from runner edges. Use a narrower border on smaller runners. Leaving the border exposed, place masking tape along chalk lines pressing tape firmly with a credit card. Paint the border with gold first, then with metallic gold. Let dry; do not remove tape.

3

Place tape on top of border leaving gold edges exposed ⅛" (3 mm). Use the script brush and metallic red to paint border edges. Let dry and remove tape. Paint red diagonal lines in border corners.

4

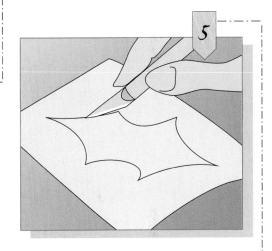

Making Stencils: Place stencil plastic over the patterns and trace with marker. Place plastic on cutting surface and use craft knife to cut out stencils. Cut and remove smallest areas first, then larger ones. Pull knife toward you as you cut. Turn plastic, rather than knife, to change directions. If desired, use a hole punch to punch several holes for berries.

5

Stenciling: Stencil holly leaves along inside border with metallic green paint, using same process as in Step 2 above. Tape or hold stencil firmly and pounce sponge inside cutout area. Continue applying paint to cover. Use entire leaf stencil, or just individual leaves. Turn stencil around from time to time for a flowing effect. Randomly stencil berries with metallic red.

6

Finishing: Use the script brush and metallic gold to outline holly leaves and paint center veins. Dot each berry with a gold highlight and paint tendrils and curving lines connecting leaves. Apply several light coats of varnish with foam brush, letting dry between coats. To clean, wipe with a damp sponge.

7

PADDED COASTERS & BOX SET

Make a set of holiday coasters, and package them in a decorative box. Purchase a small cardboard box and lid in a holiday-motif shape, such as a star, heart or tree. Make the padded coasters in the same shape as the box, using cotton quilting fabric and needlepunched cotton batting. Paint the box, and adorn the lid with an additional coaster.

MATERIALS

For Eight Coasters and Box

❋ Cardboard box in holiday-motif shape, such as a star, heart or tree, measuring about 2" (5 cm) high and 4" to 5" (10 to 12.5 cm) in diameter

❋ 1/2 yd. (0.5 m) cotton quilting fabric in Christmas print

❋ 1/2 yd. (0.5 m) needlepunched cotton batting

❋ Pinking shears

❋ Embellishments, such as tiny buttons or ribbons, optional

❋ Acrylic paint and paintbrush

❋ Craft glue

❋ Miscellaneous items: chalk pencil, straight pins, sewing machine, matching thread

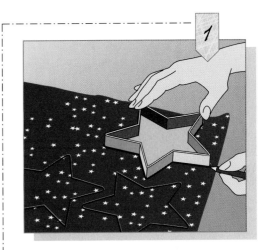

1 Prewash fabric and batting, following the manufacturer's instructions. Fold fabric in half, wrong sides together, matching selvages. Trace the box bottom on right side of fabric eight times, for eight coasters; allow ½"(1.3 cm) between coasters. Trace the box lid once for lid decoration.

2 Insert batting between the folded layers of fabric. Pin fabric and batting layers together, using two or three pins in each traced coaster.

3 Cut fabric apart through all layers, but not on traced lines. Leave irregular margins around each coaster and stitch layers together. Use small stitches, and stitch ¼" (6 mm) inside traced lines.

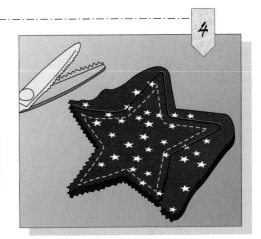

4 Cut out coasters just inside traced lines, using pinking shears. Embellish the coasters with small buttons or other embellishments, if desired.

5 Paint all surfaces of cardboard box and lid, using acrylic paint and paintbrush. Allow to dry.

6 Insert the eight small coasters into box. Embellish large coaster for lid with bow or other embellishment, if desired. Secure large coaster to lid, using craft glue.

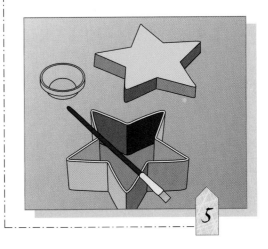

EVERGREEN TOPIARY

An elegant

evergreen

topiary laden with

fruit makes a festive

holiday decoration.

A wood dowel and Styrofoam® balls

establish the shape of this striking topiary.

Gold-tipped pine and rich red ribbon give

the arrangement holiday flair, while berries,

rosebuds, lotus pods and the fruit impart a

natural look.

MATERIALS

* 6" (15 cm) round container
* Dry floral foam block, 3" x 4" x 8" (7.5 x 10 x 20.5 cm)
* Sheet moss
* Greening pins
* Floral tape
* 1/2" (1.3 cm) wood dowel, 20" (51 cm)
* Oak wood stain
* Gold glitter spray
* Styrofoam balls: 3" (7.5 cm), 4" (10 cm); one each
* Gold-tipped mini pine picks, 20
* 2" (5 cm) red/gold wire edge ribbon, 1¼ yd. (1.15 cm)

* Artificial fruits, approximately 2" (5 cm) diameter: red apples, four; green pears, two; red pomegranates, four; blueberry clusters, four; red grape clusters, 6" (15 cm) long, two
* 2" (5 cm) lotus pods, seven
* Cosmos mixed berry picks, green/gold, 12
* Small pinecones, 15
* Red silk florentine rosebuds, seven
* Silk foliage spray with tendrils, two
* Glues: thick white craft, hot glue gun
* Miscellaneous items: small paintbrush, paper towels, masking tape, wire cutters, pencil, ruler, large kitchen knife, scissors

1. Trim floral foam to fit container. Crisscross two floral tape strips over foam, overlapping container sides ½" (1.3 cm) to secure. Cover foam with sheet moss; secure with greening pins.

2. Stain dowel with oak stain. Wipe excess with paper towel; let dry. Spray lotus pods lightly with gold glitter spray; let dry.

3. Dip end of dowel into white glue, and insert into center of floral foam in container. Insert pencil through center of each foam ball. Force the 4" (10 cm) ball down onto the dowel 5" (12.5 cm) above container. Position 3" (7.5 cm) ball on top of dowel, 5" (12.5 cm) above 4" (10 cm) ball. Wrap 12" (30.5 cm) of masking tape around dowel directly below each ball to prevent slippage. Cover balls with moss; secure with greening pins.

4. Cut mini pine pick stems to 1" (2.5 cm). Dip stems into white glue before inserting into foam. Insert ten picks, evenly spaced, into 4" (10 cm) ball. Insert six picks into 3" (7.5 cm) ball and four picks into top of container.

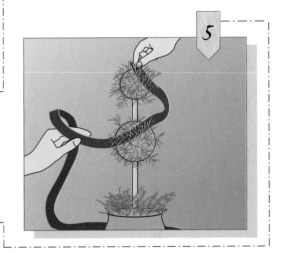

5. Pin end of wired ribbon to topiary top, then wrap and drape around topiary, securing with greening pins. Cut V notches in ribbon ends.

6. Use greening pins to attach one bunch of grapes to each ball on opposite sides to balance arrangement. Glue remaining fruits into pine, distributing them evenly over both balls. Glue three pinecones and a lotus pod to top of container. Glue remaining lotus pods, pinecones and rosebuds to fill in between fruits.

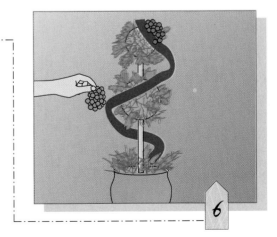

7. Cut berry pick stems to 1" (2.5 cm) and fill in topiary on both balls. Divide silk foliage spray into short sprigs, and glue into pine near fruits and naturals. Pull tendrils to loosen.

HONEYSUCKLE GARLAND

$\mathcal{D}$eck your table, wall, or mantel with a decorative honeysuckle garland. Garlands can be filled with wisps of greenery or short, dense foliage, depending on the lengths of the floral materials used. Garlands made of dried materials are fragile, and large garlands can be difficult to carry and arrange after they are finished. Therefore, you may want to construct the garland in the location where it will be displayed.

MATERIALS

* Honeysuckle vines
* Preserved plumosa or other foliage
* Silk and parchment roses or other dominant flowers
* Dried pepper berries and nigella pods or other secondary materials
* Dried pepper grass, statice, and veronica or other filler materials
* Ribbon
* Paddle floral wire
* Miscellaneous items: hot glue gun, scissors, wire cutters

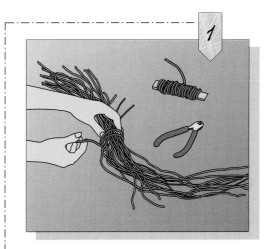

1   Cut the honeysuckle vines to arcs of desired lengths. Secure together, using floral wire.

2   Insert sprigs of plumosa or other foliage into vines until the desired fullness is achieved; secure with hot glue. Short stems make a more compact design.

3   Insert largest rose into the center of the garland to create a focal point. Insert remaining roses, spacing them evenly throughout garland; secure with hot glue.

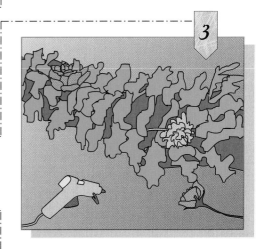

4   Insert pepper berries so they radiate from central focal point; space evenly. Secure with hot glue. Insert nigella pods or other secondary materials, spacing evenly throughout.

5   Insert pepper grass, statice, and veronica or other filler materials, one variety at a time, radiating from the focal point. Insert ribbon into garland, forming loops at center; secure with hot glue.

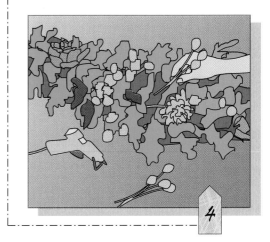

starry tree
PLACEMAT & NAPKINS

star print
fabric on a simple
patchwork placemat
gives the illusion of a pine
tree standing in the forest on a moonlit
night. A few quick seams sew the patchwork
tree design. Add a green striped fabric as a
backdrop for a place setting of your favorite
china and you'll have a placemat to use all
through the holiday season.

MATERIALS

For Four Placemats And Napkins
❋ 45" (115 cm) cotton fabrics: dark
  green/gold stars, 1¼ yd. (1.15 m);
  green stripe, ¾ yd. (0.7 m);
  blue print, ¼ yd. (0.25 m);
  brown print, ⅛ yd. (0.15 m);
  gold, ⅛ yd. (0.15 m)
❋ Paper-backed fusible web
❋ Craft batting, 30" x 40" (76 x
  102 cm) rectangle
❋ Gold embroidery floss
❋ Dark green piping, 7 yd. (6.4 m)
❋ Dark green sewing thread
❋ Pattern sheet
❋ Miscellaneous items: tracing
  paper, scissors or rotary cutter and
  mat, straight pins, tape measure,
  iron, ironing board, sewing machine

Cutting: Trace the D, E, F and star patterns; cut from fabrics as directed. In addition, from blue print cut one 4½" x 2½" (11.5 x 6.5 cm) rectangle (A) and two 2¼" x 2½" (6 x 6.5 cm) rectangles (C). From brown print, cut one 1" x 2½" (2.5 x 6.5 cm) trunk (B). From green stripe, cut one 12½" x 13½" (31.8 x 34.3 cm) rectangle (G) for rest of placemat.

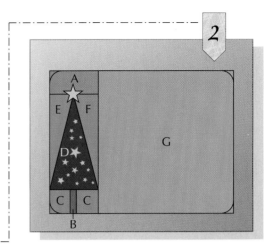

Placemat: Refer to the illustration for piecing A-G together. Sew all seams, right sides together, using a ¼" (6 mm) seam allowance. Sew E and F triangles to D. Sew a C rectangle on each long side of B.

3 Sew A to top of EDF rectangle. Sew CBC rectangle to bottom of AEDF rectangle. Sew tree rectangle to left side of G.

4 Using scissors, round all corners as shown. Press seams to one side, rather than open. Press wrong side first, then right side.

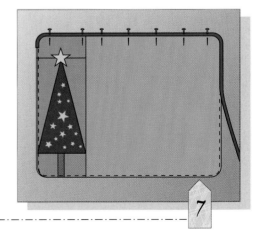

5 Fuse web to back of gold fabric and trace star on paper side of fusible web. Cut out star; remove paper backing. Follow manufacturer's instructions to fuse star to the top of the tree.

6 Using three strands of gold floss, see the illustration and page 157 to embroider a blanket stitch around the star.

7 Cut batting and backing from dark green/gold star print fabric, using pieced placemat as a pattern. Pin batting to wrong side of placemat top; baste around, close to edge. Pin piping to right side of placemat, starting in a corner, and stitch all around.

8 Pin placemat top and backing with right sides together. Sew around, leaving an opening for turning. Turn right side out and slipstitch opening shut. Topstitch around G section ¼" (6 mm) in from edges.

9 **Napkin:** Cut a 16" (40.5 cm) square from dark green/gold star print. Turn under a ¼" (6 mm) hem twice on all sides. Stitch close to edge.

CRACKLED ANGEL

*E*veryone needs a friendly spirit in their home, especially around the Holidays. But it doesn't take a miracle to make this angel—transform the precut wooden piece with crackle medium, acrylic paints, and adhesive paper on the wings. All the detail lines are done with a marker, so don't worry about painting them. This crackled angel is so cute, you may decide to keep her up all year round!

MATERIALS

* Premade wood angel cutout, 11" x 13" (28 x 33 cm) (See Sources on page 160 for purchasing information)
* Patterned papers: green/tan plaid, yellow miniprints; one each
* Ecru corrugated raffia, one package
* Paper twist: hunter green, 1/3 yd. (0.32 m); gold metallic wired, 1/2 yd. (0.5 m)
* Acrylic paint: hunter green, peach, pink, ivory, black, white
* Crackle medium
* Paintbrushes: sponge, flat, liner
* Double-sided sheet adhesive
* Trims: 5/8" (1.5 cm) tan flat button, one; mini pine garland, 5" (12.5 cm); small artificial red berries, three
* Fine-point black permanent marker
* Lightweight floral wire
* Glue: white craft, low-temp glue gun
* Pattern sheet
* Miscellaneous items: tracing paper, pencil, graphite paper, scissors, cotton swab, wire cutters

1 **Preparation:** Basecoat the entire head peach with the flat brush and the entire body and back of the wings hunter green with the sponge brush. Trace the face pattern and transfer it to the angel head using graphite paper.

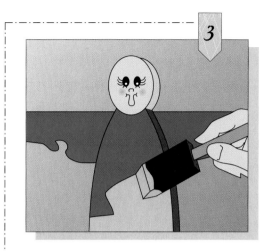

2 **Face:** Use the liner brush to paint the eyes black. Use the handle end of the brush to dot a white highlight on each eye. Use the permanent marker to draw the mouth, nose and eyelashes. Use a cotton swab and very little pink paint to blush the cheeks.

3 **Crackle Medium:** Use the sponge brush and follow the manufacturer's instructions to apply crackle medium over the hunter green body, then topcoat with ivory. Let dry. — · — · — · — · — · — · — · — · —

4 **Wings:** Follow the manufacturer's instructions to apply sheet adhesive to the wrong side of the patterned papers. Place the angel faceup on the green/tan plaid paper and trace around each side of the wings. Cut out the wings, leaving enough paper to abut the angel body on the front of each wing. Adhere paper cutouts to the wings. — · — · — · — · —

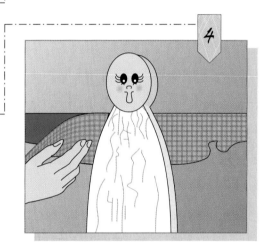

5 **Arms:** Glue one end of the green paper twist to each side of the angel's neck. Glue the pine garland around the neck and the berries to the garland.

6 **Hands:** Trace the star patterns and cut out from yellow patterned paper. Adhere the small star to the large star. Glue button to the center of the small star and the star to the paper-twist arms.

7 **Hair:** Cut and align twenty-five 18" (46 cm) corrugated raffia lengths. Use floral wire to tightly wrap the center of the raffia; trim excess wire. Cut a short raffia strand and glue it over the wire. To curl the hair, pull the flat side of each strand gently over a closed scissors edge. Center and glue the hair to the top of the head. Spot-glue some strands to the sides of the head. — · — · — · — · — · — · —

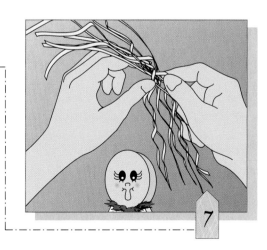

8 **Finishing:** Bend the gold metallic wired paper twist into a 2½" (6.5 cm) circle for the halo and glue it to the back of the angel's head. With the black marker, draw a dashed stitching line ⅛" (3 mm) from each wing and star edge.

Stanley SNOWMAN

$\mathcal{S}$nowmen don't come much simpler than Stanley, but he's loaded with country charm and ready to make every night a starry one. He's pleasantly plump with his French knot features, dowel nose and homespun hat and scarf. So quick and easy to make, Stanley will warm his way into the heart of everyone who sees this frosty fellow.

MATERIALS

* Natural cotton batting, 1/3 yd. (0.32 m)
* Homespun fabric: red stripe, 2 1/2" x 6" (6.5 x 15 cm); green stripe, 1 1/2" x 20" (3.8 x 51 cm)
* Black embroidery floss
* Burgundy pearl cotton, 1 yd. (0.95 m)
* 1 1/4" (3.2 cm) wood stars, four
* Acrylic paints: burgundy, pumpkin, antique gold
* 3/16" (4.5 mm) wood dowel, 3/4" (2 cm)
* 3/8" (1 cm) flat button
* Polyester fiberfill
* White craft glue
* Small stiff paintbrush
* Embroidery needle
* Pattern sheet
* Miscellaneous items: tracing paper, pencil, sewing machine, matching thread, fine sandpaper, scissors, paper towels, straight pins, pencil sharpener, drill with 1/8" bit, sewing needle

1 Refer to photo for all steps below. Stitch ¼" (6 mm) seams with a short stitch length, unless otherwise directed. Trace the patterns and cut from batting. Mark eyes, nose, mouth, buttons and star garland ends lightly on snowman front.

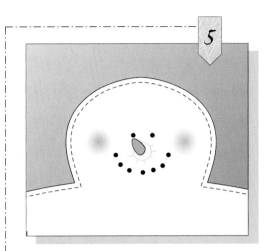

2 See page 157 for Embroidery Stitches to embroider French knot eyes, mouth and buttons. Use three strands of black floss and wrap around needle three times.

3 **Cheeks:** Dip dry paintbrush in burgundy paint and wipe on paper towel until almost dry. Wipe brush in a circular motion on cheeks, practicing first on a scrap piece of batting.

4 Stitch front and back body pieces, wrong sides together, along sides, leaving bottom open. Trim seam close to stitching.

5 **Nose:** Sharpen one end of the dowel with pencil sharpener. Paint with pumpkin; let dry. Glue flat end of dowel to button and let dry thoroughly. From inside snowman, push pointed end of dowel through nose dot. Work slowly and fibers will gradually open up. Button on end will keep dowel from going all the way through the batting.

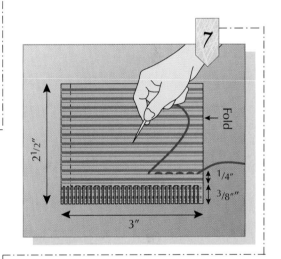

6 Pin and stitch bottom of snowman to base, leaving a 3" (7.5 cm) opening in back. Stuff evenly with fiberfill so snowman stands flat. Stitch opening closed with small running stitches. Trim seam.

7 **Hat:** Stitch short sides of 2½" x 6" (6.5 x 15 cm) stripe fabric right sides together, leaving ⅜" (1 cm) open at one end to form a tube. Turn right side out. Fringe long open end of tube down to stitching line. Cut 10" (25.5 cm) of burgundy pearl cotton and beginning opposite the seam, sew a gathering stitch ¼" (6 mm) below the fringed line. Gather and tie ends in bow. Turn bottom of hat up to make ½" (1.3 cm) cuff. Place hat at slight tilt on snowman's head.

8 **Scarf:** Fringe 1" (2.5 cm) on each end of 1½" x 20" (3.8 x 51 cm) stripe fabric. Tie around snowman's neck.

9 **Star Garland:** Paint stars antique gold; let dry. Sand stars lightly to give aged look. Drill two holes through upper half of each star ⅜" (1 cm) apart. Run burgundy pearl cotton through holes in stars, making a knot at the front of each hole and leaving a 1¼" (3.2 cm) strand between each star. Tie a knot 1¼" (3.2 cm) from each end star. Trim thread ¼" (6 mm) from knots. Stitch knot to each arm where marked.

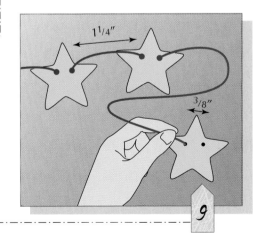

GINGERBREAD BIRDHOUSE

(Back)

Hansel and Gretel would have loved this house, and so will everyone who sees it! Gingerbread houses are always popular at Christmastime, and this one can be used year after year! Painted with acrylics, the candies look real enough to make your mouth water, and textured "snow" paint adds a sugary look to the gumdrops and candy citrus slices.

MATERIALS

❋ Wood birdhouse, 10³/₄" (27.4 cm) high (See Sources on page 160 for purchasing information)

❋ Wood cutouts: 2³/₄" (7 cm) gingerbread kids, four; ¹/₄" x ³/₄" x 2" (6 mm x 2 x 5 cm) doll house shutters, four

❋ Acrylic paints: snow white, sunshine yellow, soft shell pink, orange poppy, wine cordial, amethyst, midnight blue, Christmas green, golden fawn, hot chocolate, black kohl, lemon chiffon, citrus orange, pink surprise, Christmas red, lilac, royal purple, sky blue, green apple, mocha, expresso

❋ Pearlized acrylic paints: white frost, powder blue, pink champagne

❋ Dimensional acrylic paints: white, sapphire, gold, hot pink

❋ Textured snow paint

❋ Paintbrushes: No. 6 flat; Nos. 2, 3 round; No. 1 liner; 1" (2.5 cm) sponge

❋ Wood sealer

❋ Spray varnish

❋ White craft glue

❋ Pattern sheet

❋ Miscellaneous items: fine sandpaper, tracing paper, chalk, stylus, palette knife, old toothbrush

---

1 **Preparation:** Seal birdhouse, dowel for perch, and cutouts with wood sealer; let dry, and sand lightly. Trace the patterns onto tracing paper. Chalk candy cane trim lines only on the back and use stylus to transfer to house. Adjust pattern according to the birdhouse size. Refer to photo for all painting steps below, and to page 158 for Painting Instructions and Techniques.

2 **Basecoat:** Basecoat house, except candy cane trim areas, with mocha. Spatter entire piece with hot chocolate and expresso. Basecoat candy cane trim areas and dowel perch with white. Basecoat gingerbread kids with golden fawn. Let dry and sand lightly. Chalk remaining pattern lines on back. Use stylus to transfer to house and wood cutouts.

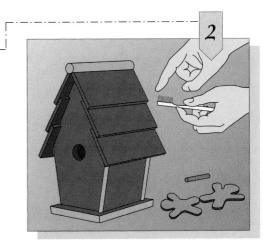

3 **Gingerbread Kids:** Paint boy's outfit sky blue, then powder blue. Paint girl's outfit soft shell pink, then pink champagne. Shade body with mocha. Using dimensional paints, add hair, features, heart on girl, and zigzag lines with white. Paint boy's buttons, bow tie, and pants cuff outlines with sapphire. Add powder blue dot to bow tie center. Paint cheeks and trim on girl's outfit with hot pink.

4 **Shutters:** Basecoat edges white. Paint front and edges soft shell pink, to look like a sugar wafer cookie. Paint front only with a second coat; use the stylus to score crosshatch lines while paint is wet. Let dry, and paint red heart and green commas and dots.

5 **Candy Canes:** Paint red stripes on candy canes and dowel perch. Add very thin green stripes to all except canes on side walls. Float midnight blue along one edge of all candy canes, except dowel perch. Add a thin white highlight along each candy cane. Paint one end of dowel perch red; add a white heart with green comma strokes and a dot.

6 **House Sides:** Basecoat the window lemon. Shade along top and left window edges with sunshine yellow. Outline top and bottom window edges and paint crosshatch lines with dimensional white. For gumdrops, mix textured snow paint with base color. Shade left side of gumdrop with pure base color. Paint gumdrops amethyst, red, green and lemon.

7 **Top Roof Layer:** Mix textured snow paint with each base color. Shade citrus orange and apple green slices with pure base color and lemon chiffon slices with sunshine. Begin with bottom row and paint up, alternating colors. Use the liner brush and stylus to paint snowflakes and line along slice edges with dimensional white.

8 **Middle Roof Layer:** Use the No. 3 round brush to basecoat each jelly bean. Let dry and apply second coat. Double-load brush with base and shading colors and shade inside curve of each jelly bean. Wipe brush, double-load with base color and pearlized white, and highlight outside curve. Add a shine mark to each jelly bean with a pearlized white comma stroke. Paint jelly beans with the following base color/shading sequence: black; lilac/amethyst; pink surprise/red; apple green/green; citrus/poppy; red/wine; amethyst/purple; lemon/sunshine yellow. Add dimensional gold dots.

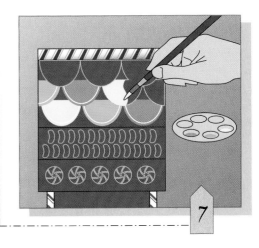

9 **Bottom Roof Layer:** Basecoat each mint white. Let dry and paint alternating mints red. Paint red comma strokes and a heart on each white mint and the reverse on red mints. Paint a circular white shine mark on each candy. Add white dimensional paint scallops and red hearts and dots across bottom edge.

10 **Roof Edges:** Use white dimensional paint for rickrack design. Paint a red heart with green comma strokes and dots on ends of roof ridge candy cane.

11 **House Front and Back:** Load the No. 2 brush with green, tip in white, and paint each bow. Use the stylus to add white dots along outside edge. Paint white rickrack around edges and add red dots. Follow Step 9 to paint red candy on back and paint stick white.

12 **Finishing:** Glue gingerbread kids to front and back of house, shutters to window sides and dowel perch into hole in front. Paint a dimensional white rickrack line around top of base. Let dry. Spray with two coats of varnish, letting dry between coats.

no-sew OLD-WORLD SANTA

For a quick answer to inspired decorating and gift giving this holiday season, craft an Old-World Santa. He has the look of a fine-crafted Father Christmas without the high cost of one purchased in a gift shop. He is a real time and money saver—he is completely constructed with a glue gun and cleverly folded fabric rectangles. Sculpt a face from easy-to-use modeling compound you bake in your own oven, and embellish Santa as you desire.

MATERIALS

- 12″ (30.5 cm) Styrofoam® cone
- Modeling compound: peach, pink, red, brown, white
- Spray glaze
- 45″ (115 cm) plaid flannel, 15″ x 18″ (38 x 46 cm) for coat; 5″ x 15″ (12.5 x 38 cm) for sleeves
- Cotton fabrics: green, 2″ x 7″ (5 x 18 cm) for hands; black-and-white check, 4″ x 7″ (10 x 18 cm) for undergarment
- Fake fur: 1″ x 7″ (2.5 x 18 cm) for hat; 3/4″ x 4″ (2 x 10 cm) for cuffs, two
- Curly gray hair or wool for beard
- Low-temp glue gun
- Polyester fiberfill
- 1/2″ (1.3 cm) gold pom-pom for hat
- Jute cord for belt, 20″ (57 cm)
- Wood toy for Santa to hold
- Miscellaneous items: scissors, pencil, iron, round toothpick, oven, ruler

1 **Face and Eyes:** Refer to the illustration to shape a ¼" (6 mm) thick half-dollar-size oval disk with peach modeling compound. Pinch two pencil-lead-size balls of brown for eyes, and place on disk. Pinch off two pea-size balls of white compound for eyebrows, and make teardrop shapes about ½" (1.3 cm) long.

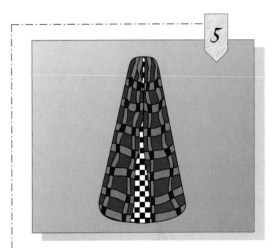

2 **Cheeks, Nose and Mouth:** Make two dime-size ⅛" (3 mm) thick disks from pink compound for cheeks, and place below eyes, slightly overlapping eyeballs. To make the nose, roll a thumbnail-size ball of peach into an elongated ¾" (2 cm) teardrop shape. Gently push up larger end to create ball at end of nose. Place a very small flattened disk of pink on top of nose ball. Scratch face disk where you will place nose. This will help pieces join as they bake. Place nose on face slightly overlapping cheeks. Make a small pencil-lead-size ball of red for mouth, and place under nose.

3 **Sculpting and Baking:** Use a round toothpick to sculpt face. Press firmly to sculpt and fuse parts together. Sculpt lines on eyebrows and cheeks and dot eyes and mouth with point. Bake compound according to manufacturer's directions. Spray face with glaze.

4 **Santa's Undergarment:** Fold a ½" (1.3 cm) hem on one 4" (10 cm) side of black-and-white check fabric. Hot-glue to foam cone with edge of hem around bottom front.

5 **Robe and Hat:** Fold a ½" (1.3 cm) hem around three sides of the 15" x 18" (38 x 46 cm) plaid fabric. Slip fabric over top of cone. Hand-gather top of fabric, and hot-glue to tip of cone. Arrange fabric in folds over cone. Close folds at center above check fabric, allowing checks to show; glue to cone. See the illustration.

6 **Sleeves:** Press a ½" (1.3 cm) hem around the 5" x 15" (12.5 x 38 cm) plaid fabric. Insert a strip of fiberfill in center, fold fabric over and hot-glue a seam. For the hands, fold a small hem on long side of green fabric. Fold over again and tie a knot in center. Refer to the illustration to glue hands inside sleeve ends and glue fur cuffs around sleeves.

7 **Finishing:** Slip arm/sleeves over top of cone and glue to back 3½" (9 cm) from top. For the hat, glue fur trim around cone 1½" (3.8 cm) from top. Glue circular beard below fur trim as in the photo. Insert face into center of beard and glue. Glue pom-pom on hat top. Glue toy in hands. Tie cord around waist, and knot ends.

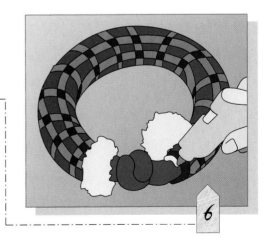

fringed FABRIC TREE

M̶ake a grouping of fabric trees in various sizes to display on a mantel. The trees are made of fringed strips of cotton fabric that were wrapped around a Styrofoam® cone. The fringe is given a frayed appearance by wetting it, then machine drying it with towels. Decorate the trees with purchased decorations or your own handmade ornaments.

MATERIALS
❋ Styrofoam cones: 6" (15 cm), 9" (23 cm), or 12" (30.5 cm); one each
❋ 1/2 yd. (0.5 m) fabric for small tree or 3/4 yd. (0.7 m) for medium or large tree
❋ Thick craft glue
❋ 4" (10 cm) lengths of wire, for securing embellishments (optional)
❋ Embellishments, such as miniature decorations and raffia (optional)
❋ Miscellaneous items: ruler, sewing machine, thread, scissors, knife

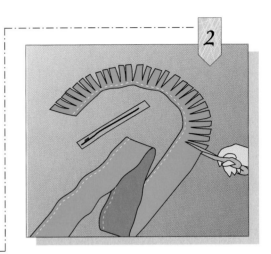

1   Tear fabric strips 4¼" (10.8 cm) wide, on crosswise grain; reserve sufficient fabric for covering cone. Fold fabric strip in half lengthwise, wrong sides together; edgestitch close to fold. Repeat for remaining strips.

2   Make the fringe by clipping the strips at ½" (1.3 cm) intervals, along the edges opposite the fold. Clip to, but not through, stitching. Wet clipped strips, and squeeze out any excess water; machine dry with towels to create frayed edges.

3   Trim Styrofoam cone to a point. Roll trimmed end gently on table to make smooth.

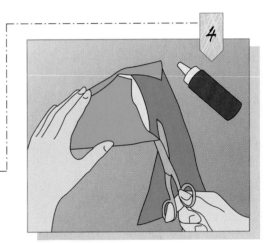

4   Wrap fabric around cone; trim off excess. Secure fabric to cone, using craft glue.

5   Apply glue to upper edge of the fringe, gluing about 4" (10 cm) at a time. Wrap fringe around the cone, starting 1" (2.5 cm) from lower edge of tree; continue to glue and wrap fringe to end of strip.

6   Continue to glue and wrap additional fringed fabric strips around cone until entire cone is covered; overlap ends of strips slightly. Trim off excess at top.

7   Embellish tree as desired, securing ornaments to tree with bent lengths of wire.

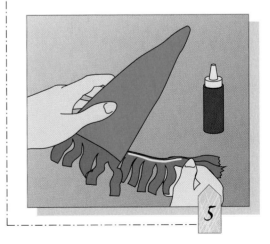

WOVEN RIBBON STOCKING

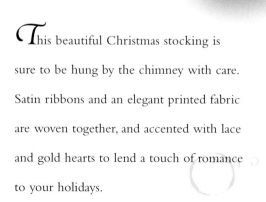

$\mathcal{T}$his beautiful Christmas stocking is sure to be hung by the chimney with care. Satin ribbons and an elegant printed fabric are woven together, and accented with lace and gold hearts to lend a touch of romance to your holidays.

MATERIALS

* 12" x 18" (30.5 x 46 cm) white-on-cream print fabric
* 45" (115 cm) teal/rose paisley fabric, 3/4 yd. (0.7 m)
* 12" x 18" (30.5 x 46 cm) fusible fleece, two rectangles
* 1/3 yd. (0.32 m) fusible web
* 9" (23 cm) square Battenburg lace doily
* Assorted gold heart charms, nine
* 3/8" (1 cm) twisted ivory cord, 1 1/4 yd. (1.15 m)

* 3/8" (1 cm) double face satin ribbon, 4 yd. (3.7 m) each: wine; hunter green; rose
* 5/8" (1.5 cm) hunter green satin ribbon, 1/4 yd. (0.25 m)
* Metallic gold thread
* Pattern sheet
* Miscellaneous items: sewing machine, ecru thread, ruler, iron, scissors, pinking shears, tracing paper, pencil, straight pins

1   Cut a 3" x 45" (7.5 x 115 cm) strip of paisley fabric. Iron fusible web to the wrong side of fabric. Cut into twelve 3" (7.5 cm) squares with pinking shears. Peel off paper backing.

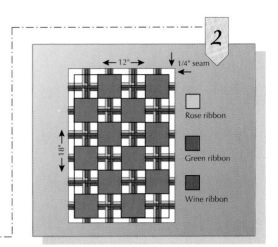

2   Cut four 18" (46 cm) lengths and six 12" (30.5 cm) lengths from each of the three colors of ⅜" (1 cm) ribbon. With cream print fabric as a base, follow the illustration to position and weave the ribbons and fuse the fabric squares on top to achieve checkerboard effect. Ribbons are woven together in the open spaces between fabric squares and lie flat underneath them.

3   Pin ribbon ends on cream fabric. Center and fuse the wrong side of woven ribbon fabric to fusible fleece. Topstitch around each square ¼" (6 mm) from the pinked edge with metallic gold thread.

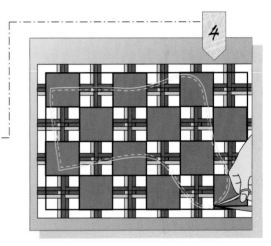

4   Trace and cut the stocking pattern. Cut three stockings (reversing one) from paisley fabric. Trace stocking pattern onto woven-ribbon fabric. Topstitch ⅛" (3 mm) inside the traced line to secure ribbon ends. Cut out woven-ribbon stocking on traced line.

5   Pin one paisley stocking and woven-ribbon fabric stocking right sides together. Stitch ¼" (6 mm) seam from top down around foot and back up; leave top open. Clip curves and turn. Repeat with two paisley lining stockings, leaving a 3" (7.5 cm) opening on one side.

6   Cut square doily in half diagonally. Center the cut edge on the stocking front, and pin. Topstitch using a ⅛" (3 mm) seam. Cut 7" (18 cm) of ⅝" (1.5 cm) ribbon for hanger. Fold hanger in half. Center ribbon ends on the outside seamline of the stocking and stitch in place.

7   Insert the stocking inside the lining, right sides together. Pin upper edges together, matching seams and raw edges; stitch ¼" (6 mm) seam. Turn right side out through the opening in the lining; slipstitch opening closed. Insert lining into stocking; press the top edge of the stocking.

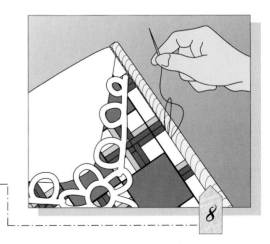

8   Slipstitch the ivory cord over stocking seam. Use metallic thread to sew gold charms in the center of the woven ribbon squares.

NOEL STOCKING

Whether or not
your home has
a fireplace
in which
a blazing
Yuletide fire
burns—you still will
probably hang up a Christmas
stocking somewhere. This elegant stocking
combines the best of both worlds—a cross-
stitched Noel, poinsettia and bell design on
a premade stocking means it's handmade,
yet quickly finished.

MATERIALS

❊ 14″ (35.5 cm) Christmas stocking with Aida cuff (See Sources on page 160 for purchasing information)

❊ DMC 6-strand embroidery floss listed on Color Key, 1 skein each

❊ Kreinik No. 8 metallic braid listed on Color Key, 1 skein each

❊ Pearl blending filament

❊ No. 24 tapestry needle

❊ Scissors

General: Refer to page 154 for Cross-Stitch Instructions and Stitches. Each square on the chart represents one square of evenweave fabric. Follow the arrows on the chart to find the chart center. Begin cross-stitching in the center of the stocking cuff.

1

Metallic Braid: Use one strand of emerald braid to stitch Noel. Use one strand of gold braid to stitch the bells and poinsettia centers.

2

Red Ribbon: Use two strands of pearl filament with one strand of red floss to stitch the ribbon. Three shades of red floss are used, 814 Dk. Garnet, 304 Med. Christmas Red and 666 Bright Christmas Red.

3

Poinsettias: Use two strands of the appropriate green and red colors to stitch poinsettia leaves and petals.

4

Backstitches: Use one strand of 310 Black floss to backstitch where indicated by heavy blue lines.

5

COLOR KEY		
symbol		color
✕	304	Med. Christmas Red
▬	666	Bright Christmas Red
▲	814	Dk. Garnet
■	310	Black
✦	500	Vy. Dk. Blue Green
╱	502	Blue Green
○	991	Dk. Aquamarine
·	002	Gold Braid
●	009HL	Emerald Braid

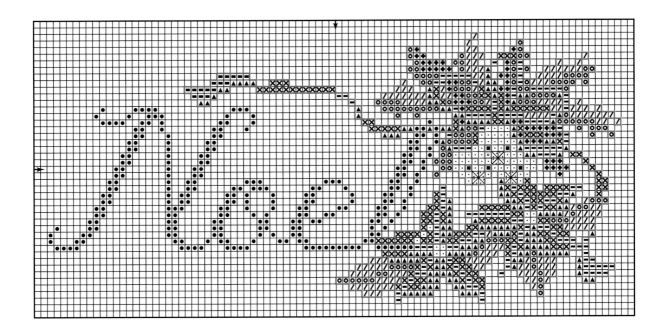

lace-trimmed & crazy-quilt
STOCKINGS

Christmas stockings need not be time-consuming projects to be special. Simple stockings can become heirlooms when they are embellished with family keepsakes, such as lace handkerchiefs or doilies. Or, use scraps of your favorite fabrics to make a crazy-quilt stocking; these stockings take on special meaning when made from old fabrics or scraps from cherished garments.

MATERIALS

For Lace-Trimmed Stocking
* ¹/₂ yd. (0.5 m) face fabric
* ¹/₂ yd. (0.5 m) lining fabric
* Low-loft quilt batting or polyester fleece
* Battenburg doily or other lace embellishments
* Ribbon, cording, or plastic ring, for hanging stocking
* Pattern sheet

For Crazy-Quilt Stocking
* Scraps of fabric for stocking front
* ⁵/₈ yd. (0.6 m) coordinating fabric for stocking back

* ⁵/₈ yd. (0.6 m) lining fabric
* ⁵/₈ yd. (0.6 m) fusible interfacing
* Low-loft quilt batting or polyester fleece
* Tear-away stabilizer
* Embellishments, ribbons, lace or buttons, if desired
* Pattern sheet
* Miscellaneous items: tracing paper, pencil, straight pins, sewing machine with decorative machine stitches, thread, hand needle, scissors, iron

1 **Pattern:** Transfer stocking pattern to paper. Add ½" (1.3 cm) seam allowances on all sides to make full-size stocking pattern.

2 **Lace-Trimmed Stocking:** Cut two stocking pieces, right sides together, from face fabric and two from lining. Also cut two stocking pieces from batting or fleece.

3 Pin lace embellishments, if desired, right side up on right side of stocking front. Trim lace even with raw edges of stocking; baste in place. Baste batting or fleece to wrong side of stocking front and back.

4 Pin the stocking front to the stocking back, right sides together. Stitch ½" (1.3 cm) seam around stocking, leaving top open. Stitch again next to first row of stitching, within seam allowances. Trim seam allowances close to stitches. Turn stocking right side out; lightly press.

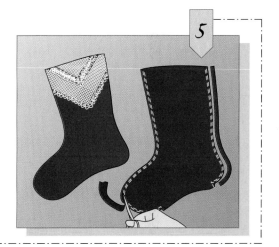

5 Pin lining pieces, right sides together. Stitch ½" (1.3 cm) seam around lining, leaving top open and bottom unstitched 4" to 6" (10 to 15 cm). Stitch again next to first row of stitching, within seam allowances. Trim seam allowances close to stitches.

6 Place outer stocking inside lining, right sides together. Pin upper edges, raw edges even; stitch. Turn right side out through opening in lining.

7 Stitch opening closed. Insert lining into the stocking; lightly press upper edge. Handstitch ribbon, cording or ring at upper edge of stocking for hanger. Edgestitch around upper edge, if desired.

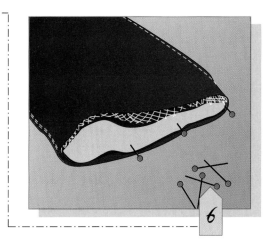

(continued)

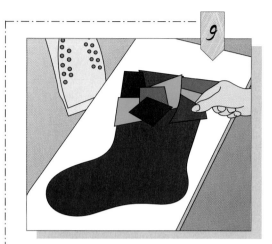

Crazy-Quilt Stocking: Cut two stocking pieces from the lining, right sides together, and two from the batting or fleece. Cut one stocking front

8 from fusible interfacing, with fusible side of interfacing up. Cut fabric scraps into a variety of shapes. Cut one stocking back from coordinating fabric, with right side of fabric down.

9 Place interfacing piece on ironing board, fusible side up. Arrange fabric scraps, right side up, on interfacing, overlapping edges. Fuse pieces in place.

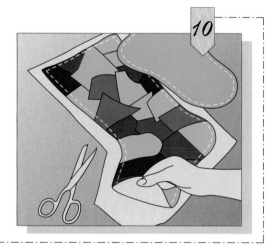

10 Trim fabric edges even with interfacing, from wrong side. Baste batting or fleece to wrong side of stocking front and back pieces; place tear-away stabilizer on batting side of stocking front.

11 Stitch around fabric scraps on stocking front, stitching through all layers with decorative machine stitches, using wide stitches that cover raw edges well. If necessary, trim raw edges of fabric close to stitches. Remove tear-away stabilizer.

12 Add embellishments, such as ribbons, lace or buttons, if desired, gluing or stitching them in place. Follow Steps 4-7 to complete stocking.

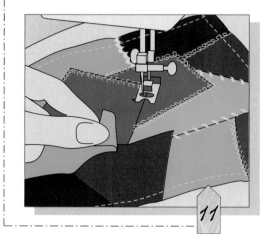

ribbon
GIFT-WRAPPED PILLOWS

Christmas pillows don't have to take long to make, either. Wrap purchased pillows in gold mesh wire-edged ribbon, tie a bow, and you are through. If you have a few extra minutes, embellish the ribbon with beads as shown, and now the pillows are exquisite.

MATERIALS

❋ Purchased pillow of your choice
❋ 2″ (5 cm) wire-edged mesh ribbon, 3 to 5 yd. (2.75 to 4.6 m), see Step 1
❋ Gold metallic thread
❋ 1/16″ (1.5 mm) green metallic ribbon
❋ Beads/trims:
For pillow A: silver beads: 3 mm; 4 mm
For pillow B: 4 mm pearl beads; 8 mm gold jingle bells, six
For pillow C: pearl beads: 4 mm round; 3 x 6 mm oval
❋ No. 24 or 26 tapestry needle
❋ Pattern sheet
❋ Miscellaneous items: tape measure, scissors

---

1 **Measuring:** Wrap tape measure in both directions around pillow and add 1 yd. (0.9 m) for bow. Cut ribbon to this measurement.

2 **Design:** Refer to the desired Bead Chart on pattern sheet. These designs are done on ribbon with a poinsettia motif, but can be adapted to any wire-edged mesh ribbon.

3 **Beading:** Start and end beading 5″ (2.5 cm) from wire-edged mesh ribbon ends; leave a 7″ (18 cm) beading ribbon/thread tail at each end. Repeat design as often as necessary.

4 **Pillow A:** Attach silver beads with gold metallic thread, the larger beads in the center and the smaller beads along the edge.

5 **Pillow B:** Attach beads and bells with 1/16″ (1.5 m) green metallic ribbon. Attach one gold jingle bell to center of three flower motifs on each ribbon end, and pearl beads to each flower center in between.

6 **Pillow C:** Attach pearl beads with gold metallic thread, the round beads in the center, and the oval beads in between as petals.

7 **Finishing:** Tie ribbon around the pillow with a bow at center of top. Knot tails of beading ribbon/thread at desired streamer length. If beads do not extend to this point, rethread tail onto needle and add additional beads, then knot. Cut V's in the ends of ribbon streamers and shape bow and streamers as desired.

The traditional presentation of a Christmas Afghan is extra special with this 50" x 60" (127 x 152.5 cm) throw worked in single and double crochet. Bordering the snowflake design are cross-stitch holly leaves accented with French knot berries for a bright and cozy Christmas wrap.

MATERIALS

❋ 3-ply sportweight yarn, 2.5 oz. (75 g) skeins: ten red, three white and one green
❋ Size G and H crochet hooks
❋ Large-eyed tapestry needle

Refer to page 157 for Crochet Abbreviations and Stitches.

1

Gauge: 4 sc equal 1" (2.5 cm)

Afghan, without border: 42" x 52" (107 x 132 cm)

Finished afghan, with border: 50" x 60" (127 x 152.5 cm)

Afghan: Ch 163 with smaller hook and red yarn. Turn work at end of each row.

Row 1: Dc in 4th ch from hook (counts as first dc) and in each ch across (161 dc).

Rows 2 and 3: Ch 3 (counts as first dc), dc in each dc across.

Row 4: Ch 3, dc in next 4 dc, ★ dc in next 7 dc, ch 3, sk next dc, dc in next 22 dc; rep from ★ across to last 6 dc, dc in next 6 dc.

Row 5: Ch 3, dc in next 4 dc, ★ dc in next 21 dc, ch 3, sk next 2 dc, sc in next ch-3 sp, ch 3, sk next 2 dc, dc in next 4 dc; rep from ★ across to last 6 dc, dc in next 6 dc.

Row 6: Ch 3, dc in next 4 dc, ★ dc in next 3 dc, ch 4, sk next 2 dc, sc in 3rd ch of next ch-3sp, sc in next sc, sc in next ch, ch 4, sk next 2 dc, dc in next 18 dc; rep from ★ across to last 6 dc, dc in next 6 dc.

Row 7: Ch 3, dc in next 4 dc, ★ dc in next 17 dc, ch 4, sk next 2 dc, sc in 4th ch of next ch-4 sp, sc in next 3 sc, sc in next ch, ch 4, sk next 2 dc; rep from ★ across to last 6 dc, dc in next 6 dc.

Row 8: Ch 3, dc in next 4 dc, ★ dc in next dc, dc in first 2 ch of next ch-4 sp, ch 4, sk next sc, sc in next 3 sc, ch 4, dc in last 2 ch of next ch-4 sp, dc in next 16 dc, rep from ★ across to last 6 dc, dc in next 6 dc.

Row 9: Ch 3, dc in next 4 dc, ★ dc in next 19 dc, dc in first 2 ch of next ch-4 sp, ch 3, sk next sc, sc in next sc, ch 3, sk next sc, dc in last 2 ch of next ch-4 sp, dc in next 2 dc; rep from ★ across to last 6 dc, dc in next 6 dc.

Row 10: Ch 3, dc in next 4 dc, ★ dc in next 5 dc, dc in first 2 ch of next ch-3 sp, ch 1, sk next sc, dc in last 2 ch of next ch-3 sp, dc in next 20 dc; rep from ★ across to last 6 dc, dc in next 6 dc.

2

Row 11: Ch 3, dc in each dc and ch across (161 sts).

Rows 12 and 13: Rep Row 2.

Row 14: Ch 3, dc in next 4 dc, ★ dc in next 22 dc, ch 3, sk next dc, dc in next 7 dc, rep from ★ across to last 6 dc, dc in next 6 dc.

Row 15: Ch 3, dc in next 4 dc, ★ dc in next 6 dc, ch 3, sk next 2 dc, sc in next ch-3 sp, ch 3, sk next 2 dc, dc in next 19 dc; rep from ★ across to last 6 dc, dc in next 6 dc.

Row 16: Ch 3, dc in next 4 dc, ★ dc in next 18 dc, ch 4, sk next 2 dc, sc in 3rd ch of next ch-3 sp, sc in next sc, sc in next ch, ch 4, sk next 2 dc, dc in next 3 dc; rep from ★ across to last 6 dc, dc in next 6 dc.

Row 17: Ch 3, dc in next 4 dc, ★ dc in next 2 dc, ch 4, sk next 2 dc, sc in 4th ch of next ch-4 sp, sc in next 3 sc, sc in next ch, ch 4, sk next 2 dc, dc in next 15 dc; rep from ★ across to last 6 dc, dc in next 6 dc.

Row 18: Ch 3, dc in next 4 dc, ★ dc in next 16 dc, dc in first 2 ch of next ch-4 sp, ch 4, sk next sc, sc in next 3 sc, ch 4, sk next sc, dc in last 2 ch of next ch-4 sp, dc in next dc; rep from ★ across to last 6 dc, dc in next 6 dc.

Row 19: Ch 3, dc in next 4 dc, ★ dc in next 4 dc, dc in first 2 ch of next ch-4 sp, ch 3, sk next sc, sc in next sc, ch 3, sk next sc, dc in last 2 ch of next ch-4 sp, dc in next 17 dc, rep from ★ across to last 6 dc, dc in next 6 dc.

Row 20: Ch 3, dc in next 4 dc, ★ dc in next 20 dc, dc in first 2 ch of next ch-3 sp, ch 1, sk next sc, dc in last 2 ch of next ch-3 sp, dc in next 5 dc; rep from ★ across to last 6 dc, dc in next 6 dc.

Row 21: Rep Row 11.

Rows 22 and 23: Rep Row 2. Rep Rows 4-23 for pattern 5 times or until total length measures 52" (132 cm). Fasten off.

Border: Use larger hook to join green to first st of last rnd.

Rnd 1: Ch 3, dc evenly spaced around entire afghan, working 2 dc, ch 1, 2 dc in each corner. Sl st in top of beg ch-3. Fasten off.

Rnd 2: Join white to any dc of last rnd, ch 1, sc in each dc around, working 3 sc in each corner ch. Sl st in beg sc.

3

Rnds 3-13: Ch 1, sc in each sc around, working 3 sc in each corner sc. Sl st in beg sc. Fasten off.

Rnd 14: Join red to any sc of last rnd, ch 3, dc in each sc around. Sl st in top of beg ch-3. Fasten off.

Holly Leaves and Berries: Refer to page 154 for Cross-Stitch Instructions and Stitches for information on fastening yarn and page 157

4 Embroidery for French knots. Use chart in illustration to work cross–stitches over one single crochet stitch with one strand of green. Work French knots with two strands of red. Begin working holly motifs at a corner over the 6th rnd of white border. Evenly space motifs 2" (5 cm) apart. Refer to the photo to stitch a three-leaf cluster at each corner.

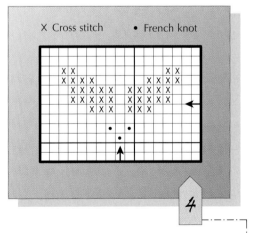

X Cross stitch   • French knot

4

TRIMMING THE TREE

What could be more traditional
than trimming the Christmas pine?
The fragrant smell of evergreen
blends with happy memories
as each ornament is pulled from
the box and lovingly placed
upon a waiting branch.
Ensure your tree is trimmed in
splendor this year by crafting
a new ornament, tree skirt, or
tree topper. From traditional
cookie-shaped felt ornaments
to elegant gold-leaf balls to
whimsical cinnamon santas,
we'll show you how to make
all our favorite tree accents!
Pick the ones that express *your*
holiday style and begin creating a
keepsake for tomorrow.

PAPER-TWIST ANGEL

*E*veryone has a different style; some begin their tree trimming with a tree topper, and others crown their tree as the finishing touch. Whichever is your approach, this paper-twist angel will complete any tree beautifully. She is given dimension with the help of foam balls, a poster board cone and wired paper twist.

MATERIALS

* Poster board , 11" x 17" (28 x 43 cm)
* Packing tape
* Three 1¹/₂" (3.8 cm) Styrofoam® balls
* ¹/₂ yd. (0.5 m) natural paper twist, 4" to 4¹/₂" (10 to 11.5 cm) wide, for head, neck, and hands
* 1 yd. (0.95 m) red paper twist, 4" to 4¹/₂" (10 to 11.5 cm) wide, for shawl
* 2 yd. (1.85 m) white paper twist, 7" to 7¹/₂" (18 to 19.3 cm) wide, for dress
* 1 yd. (0.95 m) white paper twist with wire inner core, for wings

* Sinamay ribbon, at least 2" (5 cm) wide, for wings
* Raffia
* 3-ply jute
* Dowel, ¹/₈" (3 mm) in diameter
* 24-gauge craft wire
* Thick craft glue
* Hot glue gun and glue sticks
* Wire cutters or utility scissors
* Miniature garland or other desired embellishments
* Miscellaneous items: scissors, ruler, spray bottle with water, soup or vegetable can

Cutting: From natural paper twist, cut one 4" (10 cm) piece for the head, one 10" (25 cm) piece for the underbodice, and three ¾" (2 cm) pieces for the neck and hands. From the white paper twist, cut two 4½" (11.5 cm) pieces for the sleeves, six 8½" (21.8 cm) pieces for the skirt, and one 7" (18 cm) piece for the dress bodice. From the wired inner core paper twist, cut 12" (30.5 cm) for the arms and 24" (61 cm) for the wings. Untwist the natural, white and red twist pieces; do <u>not</u> untwist wired paper twist.

1

Body: Cut a semicircle with 8" (20.5 cm) radius from poster board. Trim 6" (15 cm) pie-shaped wedge from one end; discard. Form a cone with base 15" (38 cm) around; secure with packing tape. Press the Styrofoam balls between fingers to compress to 1¼" (3.2 cm) in diameter.

2

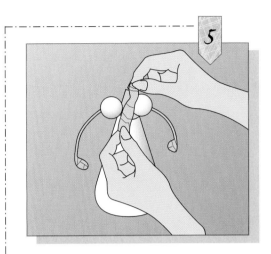

Head: Glue width of head paper twist around Styrofoam ball, using craft glue. Apply craft glue to ball at top and bottom, and tightly retwist paper. Head should look like a wrapped candy; apply additional glue as necessary so paper stays twisted. Allow glue to dry. Trim one end of the twisted paper close to foam ball; this will be top of head; see Step 6 illustration. Poke remaining twisted end, the neck, into top of cone; trim top of cone, if necessary. Remove head, and set aside.

3

Arms: Poke a hole through each side of the cone, 1" (2.5 cm) from top for the arms. Insert the wired paper twist arm through the holes. Push each wire arm through the center of foam ball for shoulders; slide balls up to the cone. Shape balls to fit snugly against cone by pressing with fingers; see Step 5 illustration. Hot-glue, applying the glue to the cone, not the foam, or foam will melt.

4

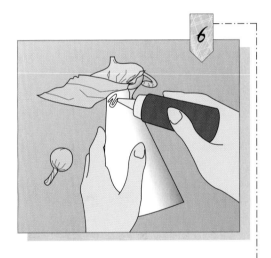

Hands: Bend each wire arm 1" (2.5 cm) from end; bend to form triangle shape for hands. Mist hand paper twist with water. See illustration to wrap twist around the hand triangle shape; secure with craft glue. Repeat for the other hand. Mist the neck paper twist, wrap around top of cone, and glue.

5

Underbodice: Cut a small slit in the center of underbodice piece. Refer to illustration to position slit in paper over top of cone; smooth paper around shoulders and cone. Secure with craft glue. Glue head in place.

6

Skirt: Join skirt pieces together by overlapping long edges ¼" (6 mm); glue to form a tube. Refer to illustration to fold ½" (1.3 cm) hem on one edge; insert wire into fold, overlapping ends of wire about 1" (2.5 cm). Secure hem with craft glue, encasing wire.

7

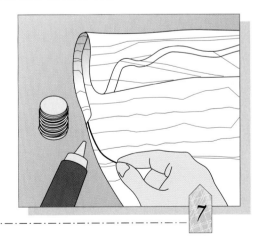

(continued)

8 See illustration to place cone on a soup or vegetable can. Slide skirt over cone, with the hem about 2" (5 cm) below the lower edge of the cone. Hand-gather upper edge to fit smoothly around the waist; secure with wire. Shape wired hem into graceful folds.

9 **Sleeves:** Overlap sleeve piece edges ¼" (6 mm) to form a tube; secure with craft glue. Fold the hem, encasing the wire as in Step 7. Slide sleeve over arm, placing hem at wrist. Glue sleeve at shoulder, sides, and underarm concealing underbodice at underarm. Shape wired hem. Repeat for other sleeve.

10 **Dress Bodice:** Cut dress bodice piece in half lengthwise. Fold strips in half lengthwise. Drape one strip over each shoulder, placing folded edges at neck; cross the ends at front and back; glue in place. Wrap wire around waist; trim excess. Cut several lengths of raffia, about 25" (63.5 cm) long; mist with water. Tie raffia around waist, concealing the wire; trim ends. Cut thicker raffia lengths, and separate into two or three strands.

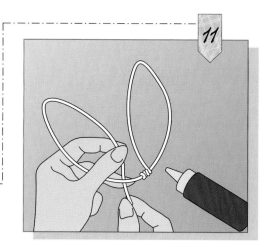

11 **Wings:** Bend the wing wired paper twist as shown; allow the ends to extend 1" (2.5 cm) beyond center. Wrap ends around center; secure with glue. Shape and curve wings as shown. Hot-glue sinamay ribbon to back of wings. Allow glue to dry; trim away excess ribbon. Position wings on back of angel at center, so wings curve away from back; secure, using hot glue.

12 **Hair:** Cut jute, and separate to make three single-ply 30" (76 cm) lengths. Wrap each ply tightly and evenly around dowel, securing the ends. Saturate jute with water. Place the dowel in 200°F/95°C oven for 2 hours or until dry. Remove jute from the dowel. Cut and glue individual lengths of coiled jute to head for hair, working in sections. For the bangs, glue short pieces across the front of the head.

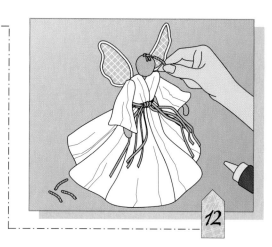

13 **Shawl:** Follow Step 7 to encase wire in a ½" (1.3 cm) hem on both long edges of shawl. Drape shawl around the shoulders; shape the wired hems to make a graceful drape. Adjust the shawl in back to conceal the lower portion of the wings. Fold the ends of shawl to underside of the skirt. Hot-glue shawl in place in several areas.

14 **Finishing:** Shape the wire arms to hold desired accessories. Hot-glue any other embellishments to angel as desired.

CINNAMON-STICK SANTA

Ornaments made from scraps are a crafter's delight, and this Santa is no exception. He will use up many extras, and takes only a few minutes to make. A bit of paint is all that is needed for Santa's face on the end of a cinnamon stick, and if you don't have a paper twist remnant to wrap and glue on the arms, use a fabric strip. Make up a whole batch of these, and decorate a wreath for your door or a garland to festoon your staircase banister.

MATERIALS
❈ Cinnamon sticks, two 6" (15 cm) pieces
❈ Untwisted red paper twist, 1/2" x 15" (1.3 x 38 cm)
❈ Acrylic paints: peach, buttermilk, red, black
❈ Small paintbrush
❈ Hot glue gun
❈ Miscellaneous items: pencil, disposable palette, paper towels, scissors, tape measure

1 Break cinnamon sticks into one 3/4" x 6" (2 x 15 cm) piece and two 1/4" x 1 1/2" (6 mm x 3.8 cm) pieces. Sizes are approximate as sticks will vary. Refer to the painting pattern as a guide, or trace and transfer to smooth side of large stick top.

2 Basecoat face with peach. Mix a small amount of red with peach, and pat on cheeks. Paint the hat red and the fur trim, mustache, beard and eyebrows buttermilk. Continue color areas around to back side, painting the hair the same length as the beard. Paint the eyes, nose and lower edge of hat trim outline with black. Let dry.

3 Untwist red paper twist and make a 1" (2.5 cm) loop in the center; twist at base to secure. Hot-glue base of loop to center lower edge of hair in back. Bring twist ends to front and crisscross. Wrap around back, then bring to front. Glue a 1 1/2" (3.8 cm) stick on for each arm. Add a dot of glue to top of each arm, crisscross twist ends back up and over shoulders to cover. Bring ends to center back, and knot. Glue knot, and trim ends.

Painting pattern

STITCHED ORNAMENTS

A

C

B

The simplest of embroidery stitches—satin stitches and cross-stitches—can create elegant ornaments. The combination of gleaming metallic gold and silver ribbon on cranberry Aida cloth is very rich, yet works well with the clean, geometric design. Because of the simple stitches and symmetrical pattern, these will be quick to stitch up for your own tree or for a friend's.

MATERIALS
For One Ornament

❋ 14-count cranberry Aida cloth: 7" (18 cm) square, 5" (12.5 cm) square for the back

❋ 1/16" (1.5 mm) metallic ribbon:
For A: gold, 3 yd. (2.75 m); silver, 9 yd. (8.25 m)
For B: gold, 10 yd. (9.15 m); silver, 2 yd. (1.85 m)

For C: gold, 8 yd. (7.35 m); silver, 2 yd. (1.85 m)

❋ No. 20 tapestry needle

❋ 5" (12.5 cm) embroidery hoop

❋ Cranberry sewing thread

❋ Polyester fiberfill

❋ Miscellaneous items: scissors, sewing needle

1. Refer to page 154 for Cross-Stitch Instructions and Stitches. Use Charts to stitch ornaments A, B and C, keeping the ribbon flat on the fabric surface.

2. **Ornament A:** Work the silver cross-stitches first, and then the gold satin stitches.

3. **Ornament B:** Work gold satin stitches, gold half cross-stitches for the border, and silver Smyrna crosses.

4. **Ornament C:** Begin in center and work gold Smyrna crosses, then continue outward, alternating gold satin stitches and Smyrna crosses. Finish with silver satin stitches.

5. **Assembly:** Trim front ½" (1.3 cm) beyond stitching. Stitch front and back right sides together two rows beyond stitched design; leave an opening. Trim edges and corners; turn. Stuff lightly with fiberfill, and slipstitch closed. Cut a 7" (18 cm) length of gold ribbon for the hanger. Loop and tack at a corner.

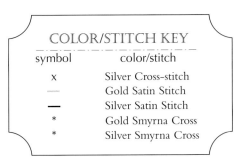

COLOR/STITCH KEY

symbol	color/stitch
x	Silver Cross-stitch
—	Gold Satin Stitch
▬	Silver Satin Stitch
*	Gold Smyrna Cross
*	Silver Smyrna Cross

Chart A

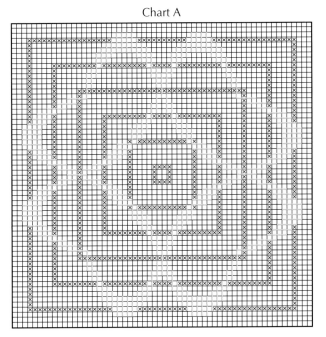

Chart B

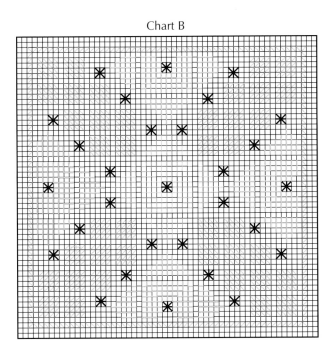

Chart C

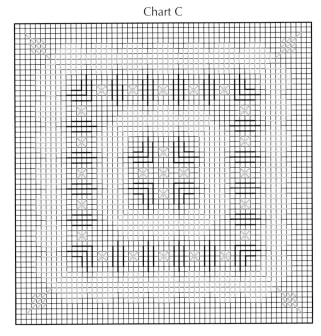

*B*asic craft supplies are all you need to create darling ornaments that will charm family and friends. Easy to paint, just basecoat the Jumbo Craft Stick Ornaments, then add details with a black permanent marking pen to make three cute Christmas characters.

MATERIALS

❄ Jumbo wood craft sticks, three

❄ Wood shapes: 2" (5 cm) stars, three; 1¹/₂" (3.8 cm) hearts, two

❄ Acrylic paints: gold, green, peach, off-white, black and red

❄ Paintbrushes: Nos. 3 and 6 round, No. 10/0 liner, ¹/₈" (3 mm) and ¹/₄" (6 mm) stencil

❄ Fine-point permanent marking pens: black and brown

❄ Red/green homespun fabric, ⁵/₈" x 9" (1.5 x 23 cm) strip for snowman

❄ ⁷/₁₆" (1.2 cm) flat buttons: off-white, tortoiseshell, one each

❄ 19-gauge black craft wire

❄ White craft glue

❄ Pattern sheet

❄ Miscellaneous items: fine sandpaper, tack cloth, drill with ³/₃₂" bit, scrap wood block, tracing paper, No. 2 pencil, palette, container for water, paper towels, scissors, ruler, wire cutters

1 **Preparation:** Lightly sand craft stick and star, and wipe with a tack cloth. Trace the pattern onto tracing paper. Pressing hard with a pencil, trace over the lines on the back of the tracing paper pattern. Place the pattern on the craft stick, right side up, and go over the solid pattern lines (except for angel's hair), pressing hard with a pencil to transfer.

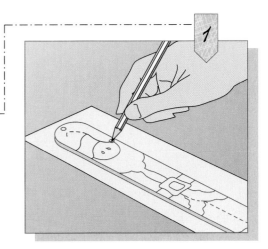

2 Place craft stick on the scrap wood block, and drill a hole as indicated on the pattern. Also drill holes in the top and bottom center of each star. Refer to page 158 for Painting Instructions and Techniques such as basecoating and dry-brushing. Refer to pattern and photo as needed for all steps below.

3 **Stars:** Basecoat the star gold; let dry. Dry-brush edges of star red with ¼" (6 mm) stencil brush.

4 **Angel:** Basecoat the heart wings, dress and back of the craft stick with off-white, head and legs with peach, stars on dress and shoes with gold. Let dry. Dry-brush the edges of the hearts with gold. **Santa:** Basecoat the suit, hat and back of the craft stick with red, face with peach, belt buckle with gold, belt and boots with black, beard and fur trim with off-white. **Snowman:** Basecoat the hat green and the remaining front and back of craft stick with off-white.

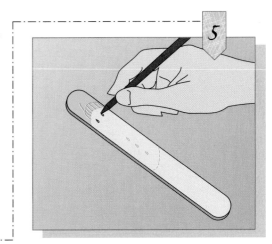

5 **For Each Ornament:** Let dry. Transfer the remaining pattern details to the craft stick. Use the black permanent pen to draw dashed lines and to fill in the buttons and eyes. Dot an off-white highlight in the center of buttons and eyes. Dry-brush cheeks with ⅛" (3 mm) stencil brush and red paint.

6 **Finishing Angel:** Draw the hair loosely with the brown pen. Glue heart wings on the back of the angel. **Santa:** Use the liner brush to paint the dashed lines between the boots with off-white. Glue the off-white button to the hat tip. **Snowman:** For the scarf, fringe the ends of the fabric strip. Wrap and tie scarf around the snowman's neck, spot-gluing the fabric in the back. Glue the tortoiseshell button to the hat.

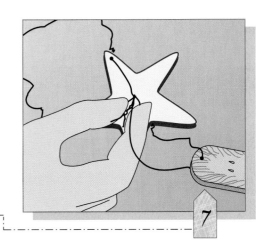

7 **Ornament Hanger:** Cut a 15" (38 cm) wire. Insert end of wire, front to back, through the top hole in the star, then back to front through the bottom hole in the star with 10" (25.5 cm) of wire above star at the top and about 4" (10 cm) below. Insert bottom of wire through hole in the craft stick, adding random bends and curls in the wire. Twist end of wire around wire in back of the star. Repeat for the top of the wire, bending it into a hanger.

RAG DOLL ANGELS

*L*ittle angel doll babies, bundled with love and trimmed with bits of naturals, are a delightful addition to any Christmas tree. They're heavenly simple and quick to make by wrapping wood doll forms with muslin strips. Just add cinnamon-stick, twig or evergreen wings, and let them naturally blend in with your Christmas decor.

MATERIALS
* 2¹/₂" (6.5 cm) wood doll forms, three
* Dried navy beans for hands, six
* Acrylic paints: apricot, rose, black, clay
* Paintbrushes: No. 10 flat, small round fabric, fine spotter
* 36" (91.5 cm) unbleached muslin, ¹/₄ yd. (0.25 m)
* Jute twine, ²/₃ yd. (0.63 m)
* Assorted natural trims: cinnamon sticks, 3¹/₂" (9 cm); twig bundles; preserved evergreen sprigs; statice; pepper berries; star anise
* Low-temp glue gun
* Scroll saw or craft knife
* Miscellaneous items: scissors, ruler, masking tape, disposable palette

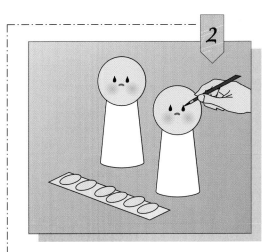

1 Refer to page 158 for Painting Instructions and Techniques and to photo for all steps below. **Hands:** Place a strip of masking tape, sticky side up, on work surface. Place navy beans on tape. Paint beans apricot on all sides.

2 **Face:** Use No. 10 flat brush to basecoat doll head with two coats of apricot; let dry. Use fabric brush to blush cheeks with rose/apricot mix. Paint eyes black and nose clay with fine spotter brush, as shown in illustration. — · — · — · — · — · — · — · —

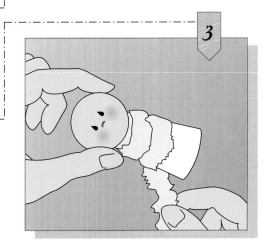

3 **Body:** Tear muslin into three ½" x 36" (1.3 x 91.5 cm) strips. Begin below head and refer to illustration to wrap muslin strips unevenly around doll body, spot-gluing as necessary. If desired, fold portions of strips in half while wrapping. Hot-glue a short strip of fabric around face edge. Glue each successive strip overlapping the previous strip to cover head. — · — · — · — · — · — ·

4 **Hanger:** Cut an 8" (20.5 cm) jute length. Knot ends and hot-glue knot to back of angel head.

5 **Arms:** Hot-glue two apricot painted beans for hands to center front of angel. If desired, fold and glue a short ½" (1.3 cm) muslin strip around hand for sleeve cuff. Glue dried statice, pepper berries and star anise between hands as desired.

6 **Twig Wings:** Tie jute around center of twig bundle. Trim wings to 3½" (9 cm) wide. Glue to center back of angel.
Evergreen Wings: Glue preserved evergreen sprigs to angel back.
Cinnamon-Stick Wings: See illustration to cut four 2" (5 cm) and two 1½" (3.8 cm) cinnamon sticks with scroll saw or craft knife. Cut ends of 2" (5 cm) sticks at an angle. Angle and glue two 2" (5 cm) sticks to each side of the 1½" (3.8 cm) stick. Glue wings to center back of angel. — · — · —

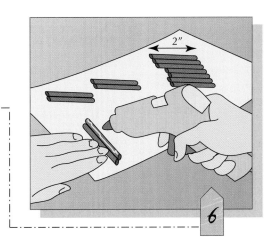

DRUM ORNAMENT

$\mathcal{T}$his drum ornament is cleverly crafted by forming prestarched fabric over the cap of an aerosol can. Paint drums in subdued colors for a realistic look or in an array of colors for a theme Christmas tree. An oil-based stain applied over the paint gives an antiqued look.

MATERIALS

❋ Prestarched fabric, such as Dip 'n Drape, Drape 'n Shape, and Fab-U-Drape (See Sources on page 160 for purchasing information)

❋ Cylinder-shaped plastic cap from aerosol can, about 2¹/₂" (6.5 cm) in diameter by 2" (5 cm) high; rubber band to fit around cap

❋ Acrylic paints and brushes; ivory paint for top of drum and desired color for base of drum

❋ Two ³/₈" (1 cm) wooden beads and two round toothpicks, for drumsticks

❋ 15" (38 cm) length of cord or leather lacing; sprig of artificial holly

❋ Oil-based stain, aerosol clear acrylic sealer

❋ Hot glue gun and glue sticks

❋ Permanent marking pen for personalizing ornament (optional)

❋ Miscellaneous items: ruler, scissors, bowl of water, wax paper, rubber bands, staining rags, T-pins, old paintbrush

1   Cut one 7" (18 cm) and one 4½" (11.5 cm) square of prestarched fabric for each ornament.

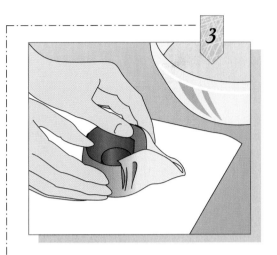

2   When using prestarched fabric, dip fabric pieces quickly in cool water; begin shaping immediately. Work quickly, and do not handle the fabric any more than necessary. If the fabric is overworked, it becomes limp and does not hold its shape. Adjust the folds of the fabric with T-pins to avoid overworking the fabric. Keep your fingers wet during shaping to prevent the fabric from sticking to them.

3   Dip 7" (18 cm) square of fabric in cool water for 5 to 10 seconds; center fabric over top of the plastic cap. Pull fabric down over sides, smoothing folds flush against cap; fold and finger-press raw edges to inside of cap. Turn cap over; allow fabric to dry overnight on wax paper.

4   Wet 4½" (11.5 cm) square of fabric as in Step 3; center it over cap opening. Place rubber band around cap, about ¼" (6 mm) from edge; gently pull fabric taut.

5   Fold under raw edges, working with wet fingers; leave edges scalloped. Let dry overnight; when dry, remove the rubber band.

6   Apply two light coats of acrylic sealer to drum. Paint top of drum ivory; paint base of drum desired color. Apply two coats of paint to the fabric for good coverage, allowing the first coat to dry before applying the second coat. Apply the stain to the drum, using old brush and following the manufacturer's instructions; wipe off excess stain with soft rag. If stain reappears while drying, rewipe as necessary.

7   Tie cord or lacing around drum, and tie ends together to make a loop for hanging ornament. Hot-glue holly sprig to drum at knot.

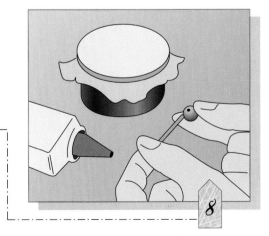

8   Cut off pointed ends of two round toothpicks; dip one end of each in hot-glue, and insert into beads to make drumsticks. Hot-glue drumsticks to drum.

9   Apply a light coat of acrylic sealer for protective finish. If desired, personalize ornament, using permanent marking pen.

QUICK-TUCK DIAMOND ORNAMENTS

C

B

A

Quilters and crafters alike
will have fun creating these diamond-
shaped holiday ornaments. Traditional red
and green Christmas print fabrics in a log
cabin pattern are tucked into scored
Styrofoam® with a putty knife, then
accented with gold beads and trims.

MATERIALS

For Each Ornament
* 1″ (2.5 cm) Styrofoam, 6″ (15 cm) square
* Christmas fabrics: assorted prints and solids, 1/8 yd. (0.15 m) each of four to seven fabrics; 6″ x 7″ (15 x 18 cm) piece for back
* 7/8″ (2.2 cm) grosgrain ribbon, 1/2 yd. (0.5 m) coordinating color
* 3-ply metallic gold thread, 9″ (23 cm)
* 3/4″ (2 cm) sequin pin
* Plastic for templates
* White craft glue

For Ornament A
* Gold lamé, 2″ (5 cm) square
* 2.5 mm gold fused bead string, 1 yd. (0.95 m)
* 5/8″ (1.5 cm) flat metallic gold braid, 1/2 yd. (0.5 m)

For Ornament B
* 1/8″ (3 mm) flat metallic gold braid, 1 yd. (0.95 m)
* 2″ (5 cm) gold head pins, two
* 3/4″ (2 cm) gold sequin pins, 22
* Gold beads: 10 mm, four; 5 mm, 22; 3 mm, two

For Ornament C
* Gold lamé, 2″ x 4″ (5 x 10 cm)
* Metallic gold trim: 1/8″ (3 mm) rickrack, 1 yd. (0.95 m); 1/4″ (6 mm) cord, 1 yd. (0.95 m)
* Pattern sheet
* Miscellaneous items: serrated sharp knife, ruler, pencil, candle stub, scissors, tracing paper, large sewing needle, thimble, fine-line permanent marker, straight pins, toothpicks, 3/4″ (2 cm) putty knife

Patterns: Trace two patterns with thirteen pattern pieces onto tracing paper. Cut out diamonds along outer lines only. Trace one outer diamond pattern onto plastic, and cut out. Use plastic template and marker to trace shape onto foam. Wax serrated knife blade, then use a sawing motion to cut diamond from foam. To smooth rough edges, rub with a scrap piece of foam.

1

2 Place paper pattern on foam, and pin at each point. Trace over pattern lines with a sharp pencil to score the foam. Remove pattern, and retrace lines to make more visible. Mark pieces 1 through 13 on second paper pattern, and cut apart. Pin pattern pieces to right side of fabrics. Before cutting, **add ¼" (6 mm) seam allowance on all sides.** For Ornament A, cut piece 1 from gold lamé, for Ornament C cut pieces 2 through 5 from gold lamé.

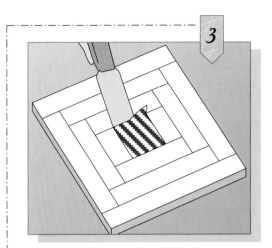

3 Place foam diamond on flat surface, and center fabric piece No. 1 right side up on it. Use the putty knife to tuck fabric edges in the scored lines as shown in illustration. If necessary, clip excess fabric, being careful not to cut the tucked fabric. Repeat to tuck the remaining fabric pieces in numerical order. Glue outside seam allowances to ornament edge.

4 Place ornament on wrong side of backing fabric and trace around outside edge. Before cutting, **add ¼" (6 mm) seam allowance to each edge.** Center, and pin to back of ornament. Glue seam allowance to ornament edge. Remove pins. Beginning at bottom, glue grosgrain ribbon around ornament edge, overlapping the ends ½" (1.3 cm).

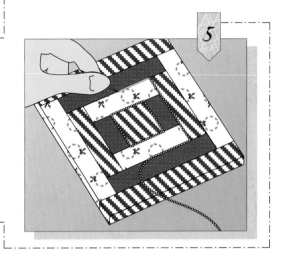

5 **Ornament A:** Use a toothpick to apply a line of glue for seamline trims on this and the following ornaments. Glue gold bead string over seamlines. Glue ⅝" (1.5 cm) braid around ornament edge.

6 **Ornament B:** Glue ⅛" (3 mm) braid over seamlines. Use needle and thimble to make holes at center of ornament top and bottom points. String a 3 mm, 5 mm and 10 mm bead on each 2" (5 cm) head pin. For the hanger, knot ends of gold thread and insert one pin through knots. Dip both pin points into glue, and insert in holes at ornament top and bottom.

7 Insert a 10 mm bead on two ¾" (2 cm) sequin pins, and dip pins in glue. Center and insert one into each side point. Insert a 5mm bead on remaining sequin pins, and dip pins in glue. Evenly space and insert five pins on each side.

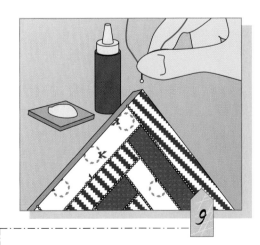

8 **Ornament C:** Glue rickrack over seamlines. Fold gold cord in half, and glue center to ornament top point. Center and glue trim around edge. Tie a square knot at bottom point, and knot near ends. Trim and fray ends.

9 **Ornament A and C hanger:** Knot ends of gold thread and insert ¾" (2 cm) sequin pin through knots. Dip pin in glue, center and insert at top edge point of ornament. Place dab of glue on head pin, and let dry.

GOLD LEAF ORNAMENTS

Turn papier-mâché balls into elegant ornaments, using imitation gold leaf. Imitation leaf, also available in silver and copper, can be found at craft and art supply stores. Several sheets are packaged together, with tissue paper between the layers. When working with the sheets of gold leaf, handle the tissue paper, not the gold leaf, whenever possible. The gold leaf is very fragile and may tarnish.

MATERIALS
✵ Papier-mâché ball
✵ Aerosol acrylic paint, optional
✵ Imitation gold, silver, or copper leaf
✵ Gold-leaf adhesive
✵ Soft-bristle brush
✵ Ribbon, for bow
✵ Aerosol clear acrylic sealer
✵ Miscellaneous items: scissors, paintbrush, thick craft glue

1 Apply aerosol paint to the papier-mâché ball, if desired; allow paint to dry. Apply gold-leaf adhesive in a small area, feathering edges. Allow the adhesive to dry until clear.

2 Cut the gold leaf and tissue paper slightly larger than the adhesive area. Press the gold leaf over the adhesive, handling the tissue only. Remove the tissue paper.

3 Remove excess gold leaf with a soft-bristle brush. Apply gold leaf to additional areas of ball as desired. Apply aerosol clear acrylic sealer. Tie ribbon in bow around base of hanger; secure with dot of craft glue.

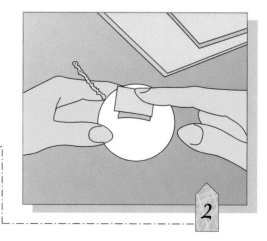

MARBLEIZED ORNAMENTS

Elegant marbleized ornaments are easy to make, using clear ornaments and craft acrylic paints. For best results, use paints that are of pouring consistency; paints may be thinned with water, if necessary. The marbleized effect is created by pouring two or three colors of paint into an ornament and swirling the paint colors together.

MATERIALS

* Clear acrylic or glass ornament, with removable top
* Craft acrylic paints in desired colors
* 9" (23 cm) of cording or ribbon, for hanger
* Ribbon, for bow
* Miscellaneous items: disposable cups, hot glue gun and glue sticks

1 Remove cap from ornament. Pour first color of paint into disposable cup; thin with water, if necessary. Pour small amount of paint into ornament; rotate to swirl paint. Place ornament, upside down, on the cup; allow any excess paint to flow out. Let paint dry slightly before going on to new color.

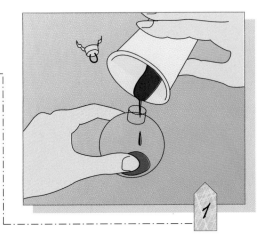

2 Repeat Step 1 for each remaining color of paint. Place the ornament, upside down, on a cup, and allow the excess paint to flow out. Turn ornament right side up; allow to dry. Paint colors will continue to mix together during the drying process. Use additional coats of paint as necessary for opaque appearance.

3 Replace cap on ornament. Insert cording or ribbon through wire loop in cap; knot ends. Make a bow from ribbon; secure to top of ornament, using hot glue.

crocheted FROSTY FLAKES

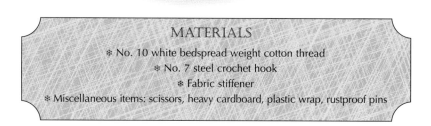

A   B   C

As quick as the snowflakes fall and cover the ground, you'll crochet a blizzard of snowflakes. Each of the three variations takes just minutes to crochet, so you can make enough not only to decorate the tree, but to use on cards, placemats, packages, wreaths, or clothing.

MATERIALS
❋ No. 10 white bedspread weight cotton thread
❋ No. 7 steel crochet hook
❋ Fabric stiffener
❋ Miscellaneous items: scissors, heavy cardboard, plastic wrap, rustproof pins

Refer to page 157 for Crochet Abbreviations and Stitches. Begin each snowflake with ch 5, sl st in first ch to form ring.

1 **Snowflake A:** *Row 1:* Ch 3, dc in ring, (ch 5, 2 dc in ring) five times, ch 2, tr in third ch. *Row 2:* Ch 3, dc in sp just made, (ch 4, 2 dc in same sp, ch 6, dc in third ch from hook, ch 10, sl st in last dc, ch 3, dc in same dc, ch 3, 2 dc in next sp) five times, omitting final 2-dc. Sl st in third ch. Fasten off.

2 **Snowflake B:** *Row 1:* Ch 3, dc in ring, (ch 5, 2 dc in ring) five times, ch 2, tr in third ch. *Row 2:* Ch 4, tr in sp just made, (ch 3, dc in last tr, ch 3, dc in last dc, ch 3, 2 dc in last dc, ch 5, 2 dc in last dc, ch 3, sl st in same dc, ch 3, dc in same dc, ch 3, dc in last dc, 2 tr in next sp) five times, omitting final 2-tr. Sl st in fourth ch. Fasten off.

3 **Snowflake C:** *Row 1:* Ch 4, tr in ring, (ch 6, 2 tr in ring) five times, ch 6, sl st in fourth ch. *Row 2:* Sc in sp between sl st and tr, (ch 6, 2 tr in next sp, ch 6, sl st in last tr, ch 10, sl st in same tr, ch 6, sl st in same tr, tr in same sp, ch 6, sc between next 2 tr) five times, omitting final sc. Sl st in first sc. Fasten off.

4 **Stiffening:** Cover cardboard with plastic wrap. Follow the manufacturer's instructions to apply fabric stiffener to snowflakes. Stretch snowflake taut on cardboard and fasten with pins. Let dry.

crocheted ORNAMENT TOPPER

Peek inside the clear ornament embellished with a crocheted topper made of variegated metallic thread and you'll find a shimmering surprise.

MATERIALS

* 2¹/₂" (6.5 cm) clear ball ornament
* Variegated metallic thread, 26 yd. (23.9 m) Kreinik Ombre Misty Sunrise thread (1800)
* No. 3 steel crochet hook
* ¹/₈" (3 mm) dark green satin ribbon, ¹/₄ yd. (0.25 m)
* Tapestry needle
* Iridescent rosette sequins, 12
* 5 mm gold beads, 12
* White craft glue
* Miscellaneous items: scissors, 4" (10 cm) cardboard square, window cleaner

Refer to page 157 for Crochet Abbreviations and Stitches.

1 **First Layer Points:** *Rnd 1:* Ch 16, sl st to form a ring, (ch 16, sl st in ring) 6 times. *Rnd 2:* Ch 1, 8 sc, dc, tr, dtr, (ch 3, sl st in top of dtr), (picot made), tr, dc, 8 sc in each 16-ch sp around, join with sl st to first sc.

2 **Second Layer Loops:** *Rnd 3:* ★Ch 35, sl st to base of ch, 6 sc over base ch between first layer points by pushing first layer stitches down; rep from ★ 6 times; join. *Rnd 4:* ★28 sc in 35-ch sp; to form loop, sk 1st 16 sc, sc in next 12 sc on opposite side of sts working over remaining 35-ch sp, 2 sc in next 6 sc; rep from ★ 5 times; join.

3 **Third Layer Ruffle:** *Rnd 5:* Push second layer loops down, ch 3, dc in same st, 2 dc in each sc around center ring, join to top of ch 3; fasten off.

4 **Tassel:** Wrap thread around cardboard six times. Cut a 6" (15 cm) piece of thread, tie folded end and slide thread off cardboard; leave ends uncut. Clip opposite ends. Wrap and tie threads together ³/₄" (2 cm) from top. Thread needle with one tassel thread and string one sequin and bead. Run the needle back through sequin, and knot. Repeat to string each thread, staggering lengths from 1" to 2³/₄" (2.5 to 7 cm). Remove ornament cap, and thread the tassel through the cap; tie, and glue to inside. Insert tassel into ball, and replace cap.

5 **Finishing:** Place crochet cover over top of ball, and evenly space and glue points, then loops, to ball. Wipe up any excess glue immediately, and let dry. Thread ribbon for ornament hanger through wire hanger, and knot ends.

WOODLAND ANGEL

This heaven-sent spirit with twig bow wings, dressed in beautiful ivory lace, symbolizes the holiday season perfectly. She is oh, so simple to make, with a wood clothespin body and wood bead head. Standing 8" (20.5 cm) tall, she carries a tiny floral spray in one hand and a mini candle in the other as a bearer of good tidings. She's wondrously decorative, and you'll want to display her all year long, not just during the holidays.

MATERIALS

* Wood clothespin—not the spring kind
* 1" (2.5 cm) wood bead
* 5" (12.5 cm) twig bow
* Auburn wool doll hair
* 7" (18 cm) ivory ruffled lace, 12" (30.5 cm)
* White wired paper twist, 7½" (19.3 cm)
* Gold novelty ring for halo
* Fine gold metallic cord, 6" (15 cm)
* 30-gauge white cloth-covered wire
* Acrylic paints: peach, deep rose, black, light brown
* Paintbrushes: No. 6 flat, small spotter
* 45" (115 cm) unbleached muslin, ¼ yd. (0.25 m)
* Ivory satin ribbon: 1/16" (1.5 mm), ½ yd. (0.5 m); ¼" (6 mm), 3½" (9 cm)
* Assorted dried naturals: baby's breath, star flowers, green fern
* Glues: white craft, low-temp glue gun
* Miscellaneous items: scissors, ruler, disposable palette, stylus, water jar, needlenose pliers, birthday candle, acorn cap, ivory sewing thread, sewing machine (optional)

1 Cut the following from muslin: 7½" x 12" (19.3 x 30.75 cm) dress; 3½" x 7½" (9 x 19.3 cm) sleeves; 3½" x 4" (9 x 10 cm) body wrap. Sew fabrics right sides together with a ¼" (6 mm) seam allowance, unless otherwise indicated.

2 **Body Wrap:** Wrap and glue 3½" x 4" (9 x 10 cm) muslin around body of clothespin below head.

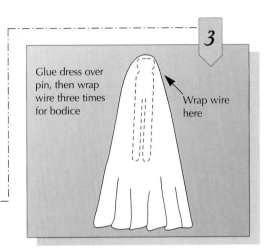

Glue dress over pin, then wrap wire three times for bodice

Wrap wire here

3

3 **Dress:** Sew a ½" (1.3 cm) hem on one long edge. Sew 7½" (19.3 cm) ends together. On wrong side of dress, sew a gathering stitch ¼" (6 mm) from top edge. Pull gathers tight; knot ends, and turn. See the illustration to secure dress to clothespin with craft glue, then wrap wire three times around base of the clothespin head for a bodice.

4 **Sleeves:** Sew a ¼" (6 mm) hem on each short end. Fold sleeves in half lengthwise and sew together to make a tube; turn.

5 **Arms/Hands:** Bend 1" (2.5 cm) hands on wired paper twist ends. Paint hands peach. See the illustrations to insert arms/hands in sleeve tube. Wrap with wire in center. Push sleeves back so hands extend ½" (1.3 cm). Wrap wire around sleeves ½" (1.3 cm) in from each end.

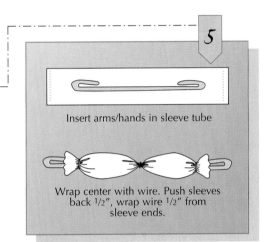

Insert arms/hands in sleeve tube

Wrap center with wire. Push sleeves back ½", wrap wire ½" from sleeve ends.

5

6 **Head:** Paint wood bead doll head with two coats of peach; let dry. Blush cheeks lightly with deep rose. Use stylus and black paint to dot eyes. Use spotter brush and light brown to paint a tiny half-circle nose. Apply a large drop of hot glue to bottom of doll head, and press onto top of doll pin so excess glue squeezes out between neck and body. Quickly wrap short length of ¼" (6 mm) ribbon around neck to hide joint.

7 **Hanger:** Knot gold metallic cord ends together; hot-glue knot to top of head.

8 **Hair:** Apply hot glue to head and quickly wrap a length of doll hair around head, crossing at center front; trim ends. Braid a length of hair, and glue across lower back of hair from ear to ear. Use white craft glue to glue gold ring halo to top of head.

9 **Lace Overskirt:** Cut 6" (15 cm) of wire. Bend one end back about ½" (1.3 cm) and weave it through lace casing. Gather lace on wire and wrap around doll's waist below bodice with opening at back; twist wire and trim excess. Glue back seam, and spot-glue at waist.

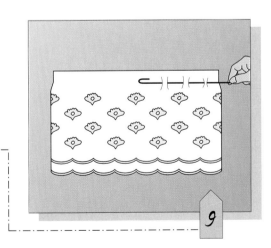

9

10 **Finishing:** Glue sleeves/arms to center back of doll. Hot-glue twig bow to center back. Form a cluster of dried naturals for the bouquet, and glue through right loop hand. Tie ¹⁄₁₆" (1.5 mm) ribbon in a bow around bouquet. Cut and glue half of a birthday candle in the acorn cap. Insert candle from bottom through left loop hand.

WOVEN VILLAGE ORNAMENTS

*C*reate your own series of woven village ornaments to give to the collectors on your gift list. You can design a different style every year and add an embellishment that shows the year it was made. Or try to pattern your woven houses after the homes of your gift recipients.

MATERIALS
❋ Weaving material, such as birch bark, corrugated art paper, handmade paper, heavy fabric
❋ Thumb tacks
❋ Mat knife and cutting mat, or craft scissors
❋ Trim material, such as paper twist, sisal rope, twigs, cording
❋ Embellishments
❋ Narrow ribbon or raffia
❋ Hot glue gun and glue sticks
❋ Miscellaneous items: ruler, pencil, awl, cardboard box

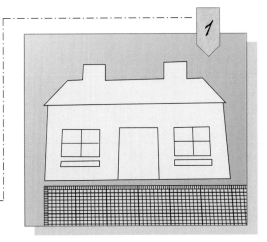

1 Draw the outline of your house design on plain paper. Measure the height and width of the pattern to determine the length and number of ½" (1.3 cm) strips of weaving material you will need.

2 Add 1" to 2" (2.5 to 5 cm) of length to each strip. For example, if your house is to be 5" (12.5 cm) high and 6" (15 cm) wide, you will need at least 12 vertical strips that are 6" to 7" (15 to 18 cm) long. The number of horizontal strips will depend on how tight a weave you want.

3 Cut strips from weaving material, using mat knife or craft scissors. On inverted cardboard box or a piece of thick cardboard, secure vertical strips side by side on one end with thumb tacks.

4 Weave horizontal strips through vertical strips, alternating rows with each new strip. The finished woven piece will be larger than your pattern.

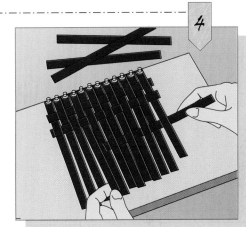

5 Lightly sketch house outline on woven piece with pencil. Cut trim material to match outline of house pattern. Hot-glue pieces of trim material along pencil outline.

6 Hot-glue door and window pieces of trim material to house. Embellish rest of house as desired. At top center of house, make a hole with an awl.

7 Remove pins and house from cardboard. Trim excess weaving strips from around the edge of house, using mat knife or craft scissors. Thread ribbon or raffia through hole in top center of house, and tie a loop for a hanger.

sparkling LACE ORNAMENTS

Trim the tree and deck the halls with these delicate and pretty Christmas ornaments made from purchased crocheted doilies. The weaving technique is easy to do—simply thread the metallic ribbon over and under alternating bars of the crochet pattern.

MATERIALS
* No. 24 tapestry needle

For the Ball Ornament
* 6" (15 cm) round ecru crocheted doilies, two*
* 1/8" (3 mm) metallic ribbon: gold, red, emerald
* 2 1/2" (6.5 cm) Styrofoam® ball

For the Soft Shape Ornament
* 4" (10 cm) round ecru crocheted doilies, two*
* 1/8" (3 mm) metallic ribbon: gold, emerald, fuchsia,
* Polyester fiberfill
* Miscellaneous items: scissors, tape measure, iron

*See Sources on page 160 for purchasing information

1 Press doilies, and work two doilies for each ornament, as follows: Thread needle with designated ribbon and knot end. Do not let ribbon twist as you work pattern. To end, weave ribbon through a few stitches in back; trim ends.

2 **Soft Shape Ornament:** Use 12" (30.5 cm) of emerald ribbon to weave a circle around center. Cut 32" (81.5 cm) of fuchsia ribbon. Begin at the dot on pattern to weave a circle and a loop in each scallop. Using 25" (63.5 cm) of gold ribbon, weave a double row of vertical stitches between each section. Bring needle up in center hole and weave through center spokes.

3 Align doilies, wrong sides together, and use 32" (81.5 cm) of emerald ribbon to weave around outer edge of scallops, beginning between two scallops and leaving two scallops unstitched. Stuff center with fiberfill, and each scallop. Finish weaving emerald ribbon to close. Make a hanger loop; knot at base and tie a small bow.

4 **Ball Ornament:** Thread needle with 20" (51 cm) of red ribbon and weave ribbon around four alternating sections of the center pinwheel. Use emerald ribbon to weave remaining pinwheel sections.

5 Use gold ribbon to come up in center of doily. Wrap ribbon around center ring and through the eight surrounding holes. Leave a short tail on the back. Align both stitched doilies, wrong sides together. Repeat above to work the flower centers in scallops through both doilies, alternating red and emerald. Leave last three flower centers unstitched. Working through both doilies, use 32" (81.5 cm) of gold ribbon to weave through the holes around outer edge of scallops, beginning around one stitched center. Leave three same flowers unstitched. Do not cut ribbon ends.

6 Insert foam ball between doilies. Use 20" (51 cm) of red ribbon to weave a circle around ball through both doilies. Do not cut ribbon ends. Work remaining three flower centers. Rethread uncut gold ribbon and weave around remaining three scallops. Tightly pull and knot red ribbon, adjusting doilies evenly around ball. Make a hanger loop; knot at base, and tie a small bow.

Soft-Shape Ornament

Leave open

Ball Ornament

MOLDED CLAY ORNAMENTS

These whimsical ornaments look like they could be made of ceramic, but instead are molded from clay. Specific directions tell you how to cut, mold and paint each piece. If you can roll a dough ball, and poke with a toothpick, you can make this cute collection of Christmas characters.

MATERIALS

For Each Ornament
❋ Oven-bake clay, 1 lb. (450 g)
(See Sources on page 160 for purchasing information)
❋ Acrylic paints: red, green, black, white, orange, brown, gold, yellow ochre
❋ Spray lacquer
❋ 18-gauge floral wire
❋ White craft glue
❋ Small paintbrush

For the Reindeer
❋ ³/8″ (1 cm) liberty bell

❋ Assorted 2 mm beads, four
❋ Extruder or garlic press

For the Stocking
❋ 22-gauge floral wire

For the Angel
❋ Gold tinsel stem
❋ Super glue

Miscellaneous items: toothpicks, wax paper, ruler, paring knife, wire cutters, toenail clippers, rolling pin, tracing paper, pencil, scissors

1 **Clay Shaping:** Refer to the photo to help shape each figure. Attach clay pieces to each other with a drop of water. To roll clay, place clay between wax paper and roll with rolling pin. Make cuts and cut shapes with paring knife. Use toenail clippers to cut toothpicks. Use a toothpick to draw lines, dots and indentations in clay.

2 **Ornament Hanger:** Cut a 1½" (3.8 cm) length of 18-gauge wire. Bend into a U shape and insert the two ends in the ornament where shown before drying.

3 **Drying:** Follow manufacturer's instructions to dry the ornaments. If none are given, air-dry the molded ornaments for two days or oven dry at 200°F/95°C for 20 minutes. Then paint ornaments. To make pink, mix a little red with white. To make peach, mix a little orange with white. When paint is dry, spray ornament with lacquer.

REINDEER

4 **Legs:** Shape a 1⅝" (4 cm) ball, then mold ball into an oval. Make a ⅝" (1.5 cm) deep cut on bottom of oval, dividing it into four equal parts. Gently pull and shape a leg from each of the four cut parts. Draw the hooves.

5 **Tail:** Roll clay into a ½" (1.3 cm) long teardrop shape. Attach pointed end to the back end of the reindeer. Attach wire hanger to top of back.

6 **Head:** Shape a 1¼" (3.2 cm) ball. Refer to the illustration to shape the head. Cut a ¾" (2 cm) toothpick. Insert one end of the toothpick into back of head and the other end into front of body.

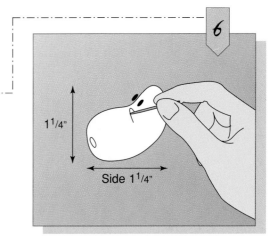

1¼"
Side 1¼"

7 **Eyes and Ears:** Shape two ⅛" (3 mm) balls. Attach to head and draw creases under the eyes and indent the nostrils. Shape two ¼" (6 mm) balls into ears. Indent center of ears and attach ears to side of head.

8 **Antlers:** Shape two 3/16" (4.5 mm) sticks 1" (2.5 cm) long. Cut two ¾" (2 cm) toothpicks and carefully insert toothpicks halfway into the clay sticks. Bend top one-third of clay sticks to shape antlers, and insert remaining toothpick ends into top of the head.

9 **Bell:** Cut 1" (2.5 cm) of 18-gauge wire, insert through bell hanger, and fold in half. Insert wire ends into the body under the neck.

10 **Wreath:** Mix a tiny amount of green paint into a 1" (2.5 cm) clay ball and same amount of red paint into a ½" (1.3 cm) clay ball. Shape red clay into ⅛" (3 mm) rope. Use the smallest hole disc of the extruder or a garlic press to press out green clay "spaghetti." Twist spaghetti together and wrap the red clay rope around the green spaghetti. Wrap around reindeer's neck and join in the back for a wreath. Press beads into the wreath.

11 **Painting:** See Step 3 for drying. Mix brown and a small amount of black to paint the reindeer. Paint the hooves and eyes black, the antlers gold and the inner ears peach.

STOCKING

1 **Stocking:** Shape clay into a 1" x 3" (2.5 x 7.5 cm) cylinder. Shape cylinder into a stocking, and draw the lines for the cuff, toe and heel. Use knife to make a ½" (1.3 cm) hollow in top of stocking. Attach hanger to top of stocking.

2 **Candy Cane and Heart:** Cut a ¾" (2 cm) piece of toothpick. Shape a ¼" x 1½" (6 mm x 3.8 cm) stick. Insert toothpick in one end and curve the other end for the cane. Shape a ½" (1.3 cm) ball into a heart. Cut a ½" (1.3 cm) piece of toothpick and insert halfway into bottom of heart.

(continued)

3 **Cat:** Shape a ¾" (2 cm) ball and refer to the illustration to shape the head. Indent both inner ears and make two holes for eyes. Shape a ⅛" (3 mm) ball for nose and attach to face. Draw the mouth. Cut four ⅜" (1 cm) pieces of 22-gauge wire and insert in the face for whiskers.

4 **Paws:** Shape a ¼" x ½" (6 mm x 1.3 cm) stick for the right paw and a ¼" x ¾" (6 mm x 2 cm) stick for left paw. Shape a ⅛" (3 mm) ball and refer to the illustration to attach to left paw for the paw pad. Draw the paw lines on the right paw and the indents on the left paw. Attach the head and paws in the stocking.

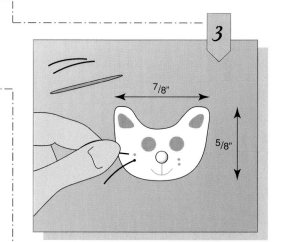

5 **Painting:** See Step 3 on page 95 to dry the stocking, cane and heart separately. Paint the stocking red; cuff white; candy cane red and white; toe, heel and heart green; cat yellow; eyes black; and the ear indents, nose and paw pad a mixture of orange and yellow. Use craft glue to glue the heart to the inside back of the cuff and the candy cane in the stocking.

ANGEL

1 **Dress:** Shape a 1¾" (4.5 cm) ball into a 1¾" (4.5 cm) tall cone. Hollow the base of the cone with your thumb.

2 **Head and Hair:** Shape a 1" (2.5 cm) ball for head. Cut toothpick in half and insert one half into bottom of ball and the other half into the top of the dress. Shape a 1" (2.5 cm) ball, flatten with your fingers, shape it to the head for hair and attach. Attach hanger to top of angel's head. Indent two holes in the face with a toothpick, for eyes.

3 **Arms:** Refer to the illustration to shape. Make an indentation around the wrists, ¼" (6 mm) from the pointed ends, to separate the hands from the sleeves. Attach an arm to each side of the body.

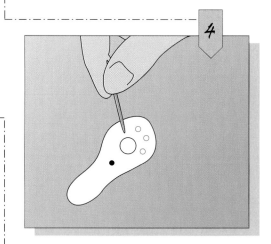

4 **Book:** Roll clay ⅛" (3 mm) thick and cut a 1" x ⅝" (2.5 x 1.5 cm) rectangle. Fold the 1" (2.5 cm) side in half and draw lines on the edge to resemble book pages. Roll clay 1/16" (1.5 mm) thick and cut a ½" x ⅝" (1.3 x 1.5 cm) rectangle. Place it on book for a page and turn up the upper outside corner slightly.

5 **Wings:** Use tracing paper to trace the pattern, and cut out. Roll clay ⅛" (3 mm) thick. Place pattern on clay, and cut wings. Draw horizontal lines across the width of the wings.

6 **Painting:** See Step 3 on page 95 to dry the angel, book and wings separately. Paint the dress and book pages white, the wings gold, the eyes black, the face and hands peach, the cover pink, and the hair a mixture of yellow, brown and a small amount of black.

7 **Finishing:** Super-glue the book to the hands and the wings to the back. Shape a 1" (2.5 cm) circle for halo from the tinsel stem and super-glue to the angel's back.

SANTA

1 **Body:** Shape a 1⅛" x 1¾" (2.8 x 4.5 cm) cylinder. Cut a ¼" (6 mm) wedge into the bottom of the cylinder and shape the feet. Shape body above the feet into an egg shape. Shape a 1⅛" (2.8 cm) ball for head.

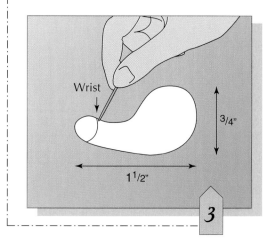

2 **Hat:** Shape a 1" (2.5 cm) ball into a cone. Cut a ⅜" (1 cm) piece of 18-gauge wire. Fold over the point and insert the wire halfway into point. Attach hat to head. Use finger to smooth the seamlines. Insert a 1" (2.5 cm) toothpick halfway into top of body and slip the head onto the other half. Shape a ¼" x 4" (6 mm x 10 cm) stick for the brim. Use your fingers to flatten and attach to edge of hat. Shape a ¼" (6 mm) ball, and slide onto wire in point of hat. Attach ornament hanger to top of head.

3 **Arms:** Shape two ⅜" (1 cm) sticks, and round both ends. Notch one end of each arm with the side of the ruler for mittens. Make a line at the wrists. Attach an arm to each side of the body.

4 **Face:** Indent two holes for the eyes. Shape a ⅛" (3 mm) ball for the nose, and attach between and slightly below the eyes. Refer to the illustration to shape a ¾" (2 cm) ball for the beard and to shape two ⅜" (1 cm) balls for the mustache; attach to the face.

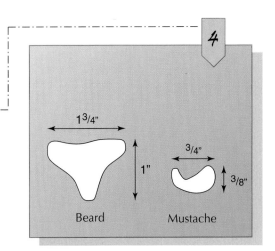

Beard   Mustache

5 **Painting:** See Step 3 on page 95 for drying. Paint the clothes and hat red, the gloves green, the face peach, the eyes and shoes black, and the beard and mustache white.

<u>SNOWMAN</u>

1 **Body:** Shape a 1½" (3.8 cm) ball and a 1⅛" (2.8 cm) ball. Angle-cut ⅛" (3 mm) sideways off the small ball. With the cut edge facing up for top of head, stack the small ball on top of the large one with a toothpick down through them.

2 **Hat:** Roll a small amount of clay to ⅛" (3 mm) thickness. Cut a 1½" (3.8 cm) circle for the brim. For the crown, shape a ¾" x ⅝" (2 x 1.5 cm) tall cylinder. Attach crown to brim. Use finger to put a slight dent in the top of the crown. Shape a ⅛" x 3" (3 mm x 7.5 cm) roll ¹⁄₁₆" (1.5 mm) thick for the ribbon, and wrap around the hat. Attach hat to the angled part of the head. Attach hanger to the hat.

3 **Scarf and Mittens:** Roll a ¼" x 6" (6 mm x 15 cm) rope, flatten it with your fingers and wrap around neck for scarf. Shape two ½" (1.3 cm) balls as shown in the illustration for mittens. Cut toothpick in half and insert one piece into each mitten. See photo to insert other ends into body for the arms.

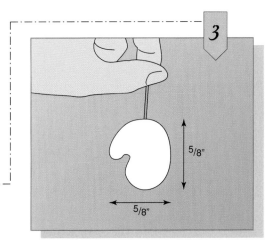

4 **Face:** Shape three ³⁄₁₆" (4.5 mm) balls. Attach two for buttons and one for the nose. Shape two ⅛" (3 mm) balls, and attach for eyes.

5 **Painting:** See Step 3 on page 95 for drying. Paint the body and head white; the hat, eyes and buttons black; the mouth, hat, ribbon and scarf red; the mittens green; and the nose orange.

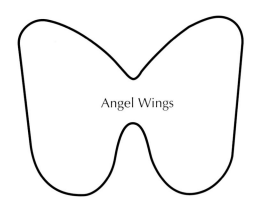

Angel Wings

YULETIDE YO-YOS

In days of yesteryear, yo-yos were a clever way of making use of small leftover pieces of fabric. The same is true today as their rising popularity emerges in the world of crafts. You've no doubt spotted them recently on T-shirts, vests, quilts and more. Stack these simple gathered fabric circles in graduated sizes to create the branches of an evergreen tree, or the flowing gown of an angel.

MATERIALS

For Each Ornament

❋ 45" (115 cm) cotton solid or print fabric, 1/8 yd. (0.15 m) each: green for the tree; white for the angel

❋ Fine metallic gold cord, 1/4 yd. (0.25 m)

❋ Large embroidery needle

❋ Hot glue gun

For the Tree

❋ 1/8" (3 mm) red satin ribbon, 1/4 yd. (0.25 m)

❋ 1/2" (1.3 cm) gold star, your choice

For the Angel

❋ 3/4" (2 cm) round wood bead for head

❋ 1 1/2" (3.8 cm) white/gold scalloped lace for wings, 6" (15 cm)

❋ 3 mm gold fused bead string, 3" (7.5 cm)

❋ Spanish moss for hair

❋ Miscellaneous items: pencil, tracing paper, cardboard, scissors, ruler, sewing needle and matching thread, sewing machine

---

1 **Each Ornament:** Trace the yo-yo patterns, and make cardboard templates. Cut out template; cut two of each size yo-yo from either fabric for a total of eight.

2 Sew short running stitches ⅛" (3 mm) from edge of each circle, leaving thread tails at each end. Evenly pull threads to gather at center; knot. Flatten circle to form a yo-yo.

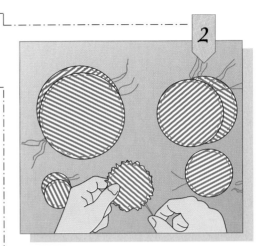

3 **Assembly:** Thread sewing needle with two strands of thread; knot. With gathered side up, sew through bottom center of largest yo-yo. Continue sewing yo-yos from largest to smallest; leave needle attached.

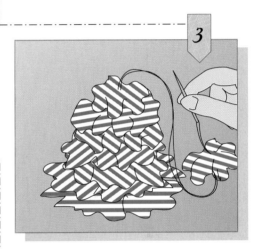

4 **Tree:** Stitch through the center of satin ribbon, then back down through ribbon and top yo-yo. Knot thread twice and trim. Tie ribbon in a small bow, and trim. Hot-glue star to bow center.

5 **Angel:** Stitch back down through top yo-yo; knot thread twice, and trim. Hot-glue head to top yo-yo, and Spanish moss for hair to top, sides and back of head. Also glue bead string in a circle to head for the halo.

6 **Wings:** Fold ribbon in half lengthwise with ends centered. Sew through layers along binding. Open lace, and finger-gather at center, forming wings. Glue wings to head and upper back.

7 **Hanger:** Thread embroidery needle with gold cord. For tree, knot a stitch up through center of top yo-yo and back down again, leaving a loop of cord at top. Knot cord twice, and trim. For angel, insert needle beneath center back halo, catching a few strands of hair with cord. Leaving a loop at top, knot cord ends adjacent to head.

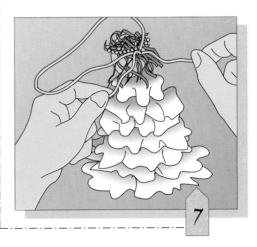

4½" (11.5 cm) YO-YO
Cut one cardboard
template

3½" (9 cm) YO-YO
Cut one cardboard
template

2½" (6.5 cm) YO-YO
Cut one cardboard
template

1¾" (4.5 cm) YO-YO
Cut one cardboard
template

HATBOX ORNAMENTS

These ornaments, reminiscent of the Victorian era, all use the same basic materials, yet each is unique with different fabrics, colors and its own painted beribboned bonnet. They're fun and easy to make, and a perfect way to use small pieces of fabrics, ribbons and trims.

MATERIALS

For Each Ornament

* 2″ (5 cm) round chipwood box
* 1³/4″ (4.5 cm) straw hat
* Ribbon or fabric: print, 6¹/2″ x 1¹/8″ (16.3 x 2.8 cm); solid or matching print, 6¹/2″ x ¹/2″ (16.3 x 1.3 cm)
* Velvet or matching fabric, 2″ (5 cm) square
* Acrylic paint, color to match ribbon or fabric
* No. 8 flat paintbrush
* Ribbon tulle or netting, coordinating color, 6″ (15 cm) square
* ³/8″ (1 cm) coordinating satin ribbon, 18″ (46 cm)
* ¹/2″ (1.3 cm) lace trim, 18″ (46 cm) (optional)
* Marabou feather, coordinating color
* ¹/2″ (1.3 cm) ribbon roses, coordinating colors, four
* Rattail or metallic cord, 6″ (15 cm)
* Small trims: pearls, strawflowers, baby's breath, sequins
* Glue: white craft, hot glue gun
* Miscellaneous items: scissors, tape measure

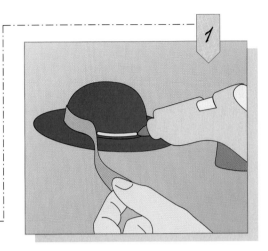

1 Hat: Basecoat straw hat with two coats of paint and let dry. Hot-glue ⅜" (1 cm) ribbon around bottom of crown. Trim excess ribbon, and tie into a small bow. If desired, glue lace over ribbon.

2 Embellishing: Hot-glue bow, ribbon roses, small dried flower sprigs, pearls and feather to back of hat. If desired, add small pieces of lace.

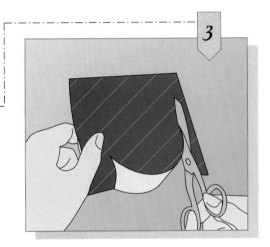

3 Lid: Glue 2" (5 cm) fabric or ribbon square to top of hat box lid and let dry. Trim fabric even with edges. Glue 6½" x ½" (16.3 x 1.3 cm) ribbon or fabric strip around lid sides.

4 Cut a 6" (15 cm) piece of ⅜" (1 cm) ribbon and tie into a bow. Place a ¾" (2 cm) circle of hot glue on center of lid and embellish same as for hat in Step 3.

5 Box: Glue 6½" x 1⅛" (16.3 x 2.8 cm) fabric around box sides; trim excess fabric. Refer to the photo and position lid propped on box; do not glue. Glue rattail or metallic cord ends inside box top, close to lid, for a hanger. Remove lid.

6 Finishing: Spread glue inside box and tuck in 6" (15 cm) tulle or netting square. Tulle should extend slightly above box sides. Reposition lid and hot-glue lid to box and hot-glue hat to box and lid.

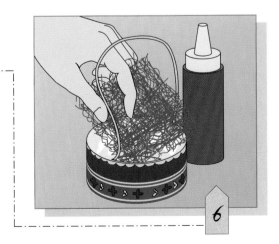

GINGERBREAD
ORNAMENT TRIO

One little, two little, three little

gingerbread men have come to celebrate a

simply scrumptious Christmas. All decked

out for the season in their holiday hats and

candy-colored trim, they're ready to spread

good cheer. Hang them among the tree

branches or high upon the wall and they'll

bring smiles to all with their impish charm.

MATERIALS

❋ Wood: 1/2" (1.3 cm) pine, 8" x 12" (20.5 x 30.5 cm); 1/2" (1.3 cm) flat hearts, three

❋ Acrylic paints: antique white, green, medium green, red, burnt sienna, brown, rust brown, off-white

❋ Paintbrushes: No. 10/0 liner; Nos. 2, 8 and 12 flat shaders; 1/2" (1.3 cm) foam brush

❋ Waterbase wood sealer

❋ Acrylic extender

❋ Textured snow paint

❋ Satin finish acrylic spray

❋ Fine-line black permanent pen

❋ Paper or satin twist ribbon: red, green

❋ Wire: 16-gauge green, 1 yd. (0.95 m); 22-gauge, 18" (46 cm)

❋ Tools: jig saw, drill with 3/32" bit

❋ White craft glue

❋ Pattern sheet

❋ Miscellaneous items: tracing paper, pencil, graphite paper, stylus, fine sandpaper, tack cloth, brown paper bag, disposable palette, paper towels, old scruffy soft paintbrush, palette knife, wire cutters

1 Trace the patterns; use graphite paper and a stylus to transfer the outlines only to the pine. Cut out the wood shapes and sand to smooth. Drill ¼" (6 mm) deep holes into the side of each ornament where indicated. Wipe with a tack cloth. Brush on wood sealer; let dry. Rub wood with brown paper bag to smooth.

2 Refer to page 158 for Painting Instructions and Techniques, including basecoating, shading and highlighting.

3 **Basecoating:** Use ½" (1.3 cm) foam brush to basecoat hearts and body fronts and backs with antique white, body edges with rust brown, hat on A with green and hat on B with red.

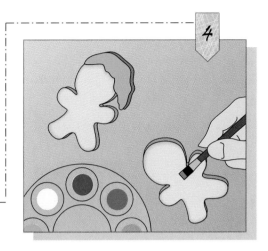

4 **Shading:** Use No. 8 brush to shade arms, legs and across top of head with burnt sienna. Repeat with brown to deepen color. Shade the green hat with medium green and the red hat with brown.

5 **Highlighting:** Use liner brush to highlight the red hat with off-white. Mix two parts green with one part off-white to highlight the green hat. Let dry.

6 Use the graphite paper and a stylus to transfer the remaining pattern details to the ornaments.

7 **Eyes:** For A and C, fill in the eyes with black. Shade along the outer edge with brown and the inner edge with off-white. Highlight with a dot of off-white. Use the liner brush to paint black eyelashes. For B, use the liner brush to paint the eyes and eyelashes black. Highlight underneath the lashes with off-white.

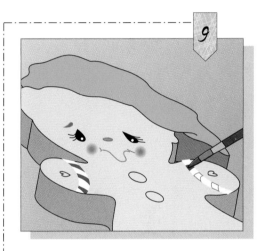

8 **Face:** Use a wash of burnt sienna for the nose. Use the liner and burnt sienna to outline the nose and paint the mouth. Dry-brush cheeks with red and old scruffy paintbrush. Paint small rust brown comma strokes for eyebrows and hair on B.

9 **Details for A and C:** Basecoat the wrist and leg bands with off-white and paint the stripes red. Shade along the inside edge of each band with burnt sienna. Outline each band with pen. Paint the hearts on hands and feet with green. Paint the buttons green and highlight with off-white. On C, paint bow with the liner brush and green. Shade under neckline with burnt sienna. Paint red hearts on cheeks and forehead.

10 **Details for B:** Use the liner brush to paint green squiggly lines for arm and leg cuffs. Use red for hearts on the hands and feet. Paint buttons off-white and use the liner brush to paint red swirls. Outline with pen.

11 **Finishing:** Use the stylus to add trios of off-white dots to the front of each body. Apply snow paint to the hat brims with the palette knife. Let dry. Spray each ornament with acrylic sealer; let dry.

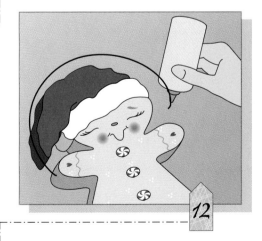

12 **Assembly:** Cut and evenly bend 11" (28 cm) of 16-gauge wire into a circular shape. Glue each wire end into the drilled hole on each side of the ornament. Let dry. Cut 12" (30.5 cm) of ribbon and tie into a 3" (7.5 cm) bow. Use 22-gauge wire to secure and attach the bow to the wire hanger; spot-glue. Trim the streamer ends. Glue a ½" (1.3 cm) heart to the bow center. Let dry.

FABRIC-TRIMMED ORNAMENTS

Create elegant ornaments by covering Styrofoam® balls with rich fabrics and trims. Four wedge-shaped fabric pieces are used to cover the Styrofoam ball. Use one fabric, or select up to four different coordinating fabrics. Glue the fabric pieces to the ball, and conceal the raw edges with flat trim, such as ribbon or braid. Cording, pearls, sequins or beads can also be used to embellish the ornament. The hanger of the ornament is made from a decorative cord and an ornamental cap.

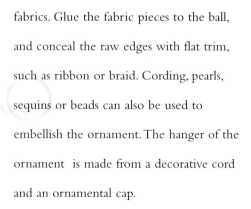

MATERIALS
❋ 3" (7.5 cm) Styrofoam ball
❋ Fabric scraps
❋ Cording and flat trims, such as ribbon or braid
❋ Decorative beads, pearls, sequins and bead pin (optional)
❋ 9" (23 cm) length of cording and ornamental cap, for hanger
❋ Thick craft glue; hot glue gun and glue sticks
❋ Miscellaneous items: tracing paper, pencil, scissors

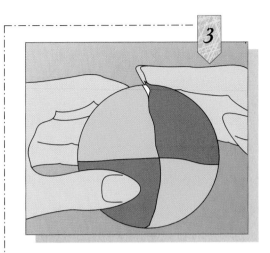

1 Trace the pattern, and cut four pieces from fabric scraps.

2 Apply craft glue near the edges on the wrong side of one fabric piece. Position the fabric piece on Styrofoam ball; smooth edges around the ball, easing fullness along sides.

3 Apply remaining fabric pieces to ball; match points and align raw edges to cover ball completely. —————————————————

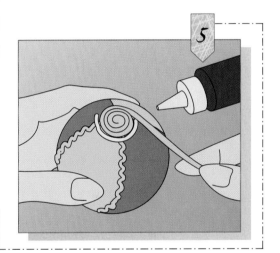

4 Glue trim over the raw edges of the fabric pieces, butting raw edges of trim at top of ornament.

5 Poke hole in Styrofoam ball at top of ornament. Insert end of one or two pieces of cording into hole; secure with craft glue. Apply glue to fabric as shown; wrap the cording tightly around the ball in one continuous spiral, until desired effect is achieved. Poke end of cording into Styrofoam; secure with glue. —·—·—·—·

6 Embellish with additional cording, if desired. Attach decorative beads, pearls and sequins, if desired, using bead pins; secure with dots of craft glue.

7 Insert cord in decorative cap; knot ends. Shape cap to fit top of ornament; secure with hot glue. Add bead or decorative cap to bottom, if desired. —·—·—·—

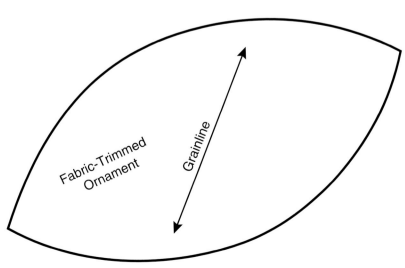

Fabric-Trimmed Ornament

Grainline

HARDANGER TREE ORNAMENT

Norway's Hardanger embroidery is traditionally done with white thread, but this Christmas tree ornament is appropriately done in green. Hardanger, with its lacy spiderweb cutouts, only looks intimidating to do. Simple blocks of satin stitches alternate vertically and horizontally to bind stitches for the cutout areas, or are filled in with red, yellow and orange eyelet stitches for ornaments.

MATERIALS

* Hardanger fabric, 6" (15 cm) square
* White cotton fabric, 6" (15 cm) square
* No. 5 pearl cotton: green (701), white
* No. 8 green (701) pearl cotton
* Embroidery floss: red, yellow, orange
* No. 22 tapestry needle
* Low-loft batting, 6" (15 cm) square
* 1/2" (1.3 cm) white ruffled lace, 1/2 yd. (0.5 m)
* Miscellaneous items: sharp-pointed scissors, two 6" (15 cm) squares lightweight cardboard, aluminum foil, sewing needle, matching thread, pencil

1 Refer to page 155 for Hardanger Instructions and Stitches. Each square on the Chart represents two threads of Hardanger fabric.

2 **Kloster Blocks:** Fold fabric in half vertically to determine center. Begin at top of tree 1¼" (3.2 cm) from top of fabric and two threads left of center. Use No. 5 green pearl cotton and work Kloster block on top of tree; continue working Kloster blocks down tree. Take care when moving from block to block that the thread will not run across areas of fabric that you will cut. You run the risk of cutting the stitched threads and unraveling your work, or of the stitched thread showing through the cutouts.

3 **Eyelets:** Work with one strand of floss, changing colors for A, B, and C. When complete, insert a large-eyed needle into centers to make uniform openings.

4 **Cutting:** Make cuts along dotted cutting lines shown on Chart. Bring scissors point out of fabric as you cut each fabric thread one at a time. Gently pull and remove cut fabric threads.

5 **Woven Bars and Dove's Eyes:** Use one strand No. 8 green pearl cotton and work as shown in illustrations. When weaving, pull stitches snugly, pulling upward to right after a left-hand stitch and upward to left after a right-hand stitch.

6 **Ornament Assembly:** Cut two 6" (15 cm) cardboard circles. Place batting, foil and Hardanger embroidery right side up on one cardboard circle. Lace thread back and forth across back of cardboard, firmly holding all fabrics in place. Backstitch around the edge of the ornament to remove fabric puckers. Repeat to cover and lace other cardboard with white cotton fabric. Baste lace around outer back edge of front, and slipstitch back and front together.

7 **Hanging Loop:** Cut a length of white pearl cotton 4½ times the distance around the ornament. Knot the two ends together. Fasten one end of the doubled thread to a doorknob. Insert pencil in opposite looped end and twist until thread kinks. Remove the pencil, and knot ends together. Fold twisted cord back on itself to form a cord. Tack twisted cord around front edge of ornament at base of the lace, leaving loop at top for hanger. Pull hanger to back through lace.

STITCH KEY

▥▤	Kloster Blocks - Note Direction
▨▧	Woven Bars - Note Direction
....	Cutting Four Threads
⊞	Dove's Eye
A	Red Eyelet
B	Orange Eyelet
C	Yellow Eyelet

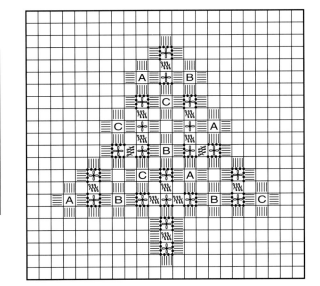

STRING BALL ORNAMENTS

Oversized string balls filled with nothing
but air seem to magically keep their shape.
An ornament is created by wrapping a
balloon with string and decorative cords or
narrow ribbons, then applying a liquid
fabric stiffener and allowing it to dry. When
the balloon is popped and removed, the
stiffened string ball can be decorated with
ribbons and other embellishments.

MATERIALS

* Round latex balloons, in desired sizes
* Liquid fabric stiffener
* Foam brush
* Wrapping materials, such as string, metallic cord, narrow braid, and narrow ribbon
* Embellishments, such as glitter, sequins, and confetti (optional)
* Metallic cord, for hanger

* Ribbon, for bows
* Clothespins, dowel 3/8" (1 cm) or smaller in diameter, and deep cardboard box, for suspending wet balloon
* Miscellaneous items: scissors, large-eyed needle, straight pin, pencil

1   Inflate balloon to desired size; knot end. Grasp balloon by the knot; apply thin
    layer of liquid fabric stiffener to entire surface of balloon, using foam applicator.

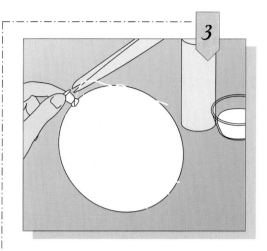

2   Wrap end of string loosely around base of knot. Wrap string around
    balloon and back to knot.

3   Continue to wrap string around the balloon, changing directions gradually;
    sparsely cover entire surface of balloon. Wrap string loosely around knot; cut
    string. Apply another layer of fabric stiffener to string.

4   Repeat Steps 2 and 3 for each additional layer of wrapping material.
    Continue to add layers of string until surface of balloon is evenly covered
    to desired density.

5   Apply generous coat of liquid fabric stiffener over the entire wrapped balloon.
    Sprinkle with glitter, if desired.

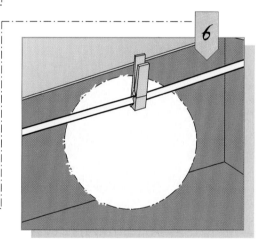

6   Suspend balloon from dowel using clothespin. Prop dowel across opening
    of deep cardboard box, allowing balloon to drip into box. Allow to dry
    completely.

7   Pop balloon; loosen any areas of balloon that may stick, using eraser end of
    pencil. Pull deflated balloon out of the ball through hole left by balloon knot
    at top. Remove any remaining residue between strings with eraser end of pencil
    or a pin.

8   Attach cord at top of ball, using large-eyed needle. Insert needle into hole
    left by balloon knot, and exit through any space, about ½" (1.3 cm) away.
    Knot ends of cord to form loop for hanging.

9   Insert ribbons into same holes as cord; tie into bows. Embellish ornament
    as desired.

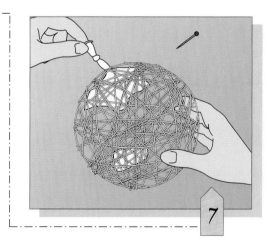

FELT COOKIE ORNAMENTS

Close your eyes and think of Christmas. Before you know it, you can almost smell gingerbread baking. Craft a lasting reminder of the fragrant aroma with a plateful of no-calorie felt cookie ornaments. Off-white yarn couched on tan felt looks just like icing on gingerbread cookies, but for even faster ornaments, simply glue the yarn on rather than embroidering it on.

MATERIALS
❋ 9" x 12" (23 x 30.5 cm) tan felt, two sheets
❋ Off-white worsted weight yarn
❋ Embroidery floss: off-white, tan
❋ Polyester fiberfill
❋ Needles: sewing, large-eyed sewing
❋ Miscellaneous items: tracing and transfer paper, pencil, scissors, matching thread

1 Trace the patterns and cut two of each from felt. See page 157 Embroidery Stitches for French knot and couching illustrations.

2 Couch a yarn outline ³⁄₁₆" (4.5 mm) from edge of ornament front using three strands of off-white floss. On gingerbread man, use one strand of yarn for French knot eyes and buttons.

3 Whipstitch front to back, leaving a small opening. Stuff lightly with fiberfill, and whipstitch closed. Use tan floss to make a hanging loop at top of ornament.

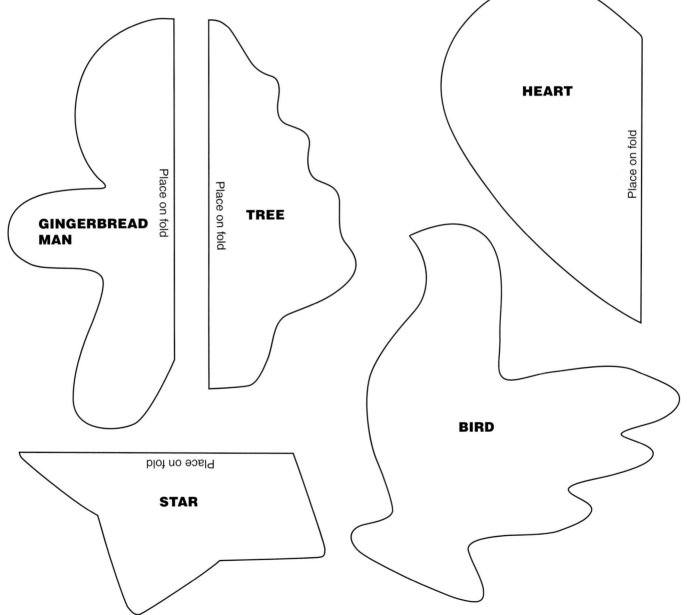

STAR TREE SKIRT

*C*omplete your Christmas tree with this star-embellished tree skirt you can make in a twinkling. Make it with purchased quilted fabric, then simply fuse on the fabric stars. Then stitch on the eyelet, glue the rickrack, and tack on the charms and ribbons. It's so pretty, you'll almost hate to pile up the presents underneath the tree.

MATERIALS

* 45" (115 cm) red quilted fabric, 1¼ yd. (1.15 m)
* White cotton fabric with gold star print, ¼ yd. (0.25 m)
* Paper-backed fusible web, ⅓ yd. (0.32 m)
* 3½" (9 cm) white ruffled eyelet, 4 yd. (3.7 m)
* ¹⁄₁₆" (1.5 mm) white satin ribbon, 6 yd. (5.5 m)
* Metallic multicolor rickrack, 4 yd. (3.7 m)
* Red double-fold bias tape, one package
* Assorted gold star charms, 24
* Lightweight string, 1 yd. (0.95 m)
* Darning needle
* Fabric glue
* Pattern sheet
* Miscellaneous items: sewing machine, iron, scissors, white chalk, tracing paper, pencil, tape measure, cardboard, straight pins

1   Fold red quilted fabric in half lengthwise, then crosswise, to make a square. Tie one end of string to chalk, then knot string 22" (56 cm) from chalk. Place knot at folded corner of fabric, and position chalk at cut edge of fabric. Holding knot firmly and keeping string taut, draw an arc.

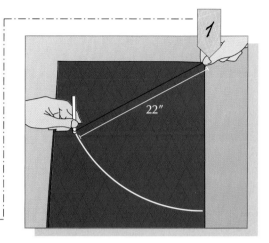

2   Untie chalk from string and retie chalk 2" (5 cm) from knot. Repeat to draw a small arc in corner for center opening. Cut fabric along both arcs, cutting large one first. Open circle, then fold in half. Cut along foldline from one edge to center to make back opening.

3   Pin bias tape to back edges and center opening of tree skirt, with right sides together and raw edges matching. Stitch along the first foldline of the bias tape. Clip seam allowances around the center circle; trim corners. Press bias tape to wrong side of skirt; pin in place, mitering tape at corners. Sew eyelet around outside edge of skirt on right side. Glue rickrack to cover bound edge of eyelet.

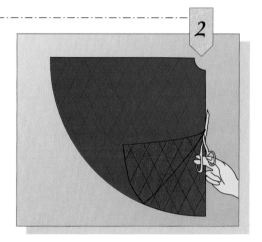

4   Follow manufacturer's instructions to fuse web to wrong side of cotton fabric. Trace the star patterns onto tracing paper, and cut from cardboard. Use the cardboard star templates to draw seven large, fourteen medium, and twelve small stars on paper backing of fusible web. Cut out stars, and refer to the photo to fuse randomly to skirt.

5   Cut ribbon into twenty-four 9" (23 cm) pieces. Use a darning needle to sew ribbon ends through skirt from front to back, with about ¼" (6 mm) between ends. Attach a charm to each ribbon, and tie ribbon ends into a bow. Add a dot of glue to center of each bow.

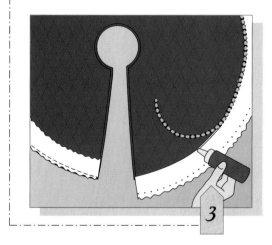

LAYERED TREE SKIRT

Decorate the base of a Christmas tree with a layered tree skirt embellished with ribbon bows. When arranged around the tree, it resembles an eight-pointed star. Easy to make, it is simply two lined squares of fabric, stitched together around center openings.

MATERIALS
* 1¼ yd. (1.15 m) each, of two coordinating fabrics
* 1¼ yd. (1.15 m) each, of two solid-color lining fabrics
* Eight large safety pins
* Wired ribbon
* Miscellaneous items: ruler, chalk pencil, scissors, straight pins, sewing machine, thread

1 Cut outer fabric into a square, trimming selvages. Fold fabric in half lengthwise, then crosswise. Mark an arc, measuring 1¾" (4.5 cm) from folded center of fabric. Cut on marked line. Pin-mark one folded edge at raw outer edges for the center back opening.

2 Open fabric and mark cutting line from outer raw edge to center opening, on wrong side of fabric.

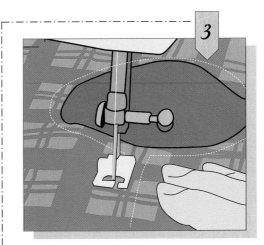

3 Place face fabric on lining, right sides together; pin the layers together. Stitch ¼" (6 mm) seam around tree skirt, stitching around all edges and on each side of center back line. Leave 6" (15 cm) opening for turning along one side of center back. For sheer fabrics, stitch a second row scant ⅛" (3 mm) from first stitching.

4 Cut on marked line; trim lining even with edges of outer fabric. Clip seam allowances around center circle; trim corners diagonally. Turn right side out; press. Slipstitch opening closed.

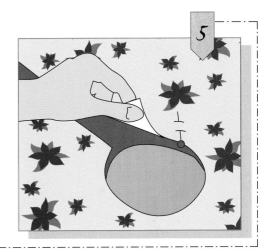

5 Repeat Steps 1 to 4 for the other tree skirt layer. Align skirts, right sides up, matching center back openings. Shift the upper skirt so corners of the lower skirt are centered at sides of upper skirt. Pin-mark opening of lower skirt on upper skirt. Pin layers together around the center from marked point to opening in the upper skirt.

6 Topstitch ¼" (6 mm) from the raw edges around center, from opening to marked point, securing the two tree skirt layers together.

7 Gather and bunch fabric at the center of one long edge by inserting point of safety pin in and out of fabric for about 6" (15 cm) on lining side of the tree skirt; close the pin. Repeat at center of each side for each tree skirt layer; do not pin back opening sides.

8 Place skirt around base of tree. Overlap back opening at outer edge; gather and bunch fabric for underlayer with safety pin. Repeat for remaining center back opening of upper layer of skirt.

9 Make four ribbon bows. Position a bow at each side of the upper layer, concealing safety pin. Secure with pin or tack in place.

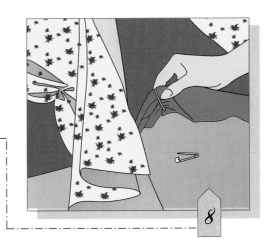

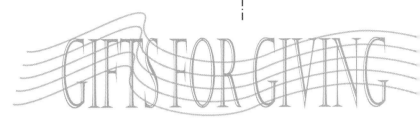

GIFTS FOR GIVING

Share your holiday spirit with
loved ones by creating
an original handcrafted gift
just for them!
Our collection of
yuletide treasures will appeal
to everyone on your list.
Whether an adorable holiday vest
or an elegant decoupage plate
heaped with a batch of warm
homemade cookies, a
handcrafted goodie under
the tree will be welcomed
by family and friends.
As an added touch,
create unique cards, trims,
bags and tags to make your gift
one-of-a-kind
both inside and out.

DECOUPAGE PLATES

A favorite gift for holiday time is a plateful of homemade goodies. Add to this special gift by presenting your treats on a decorative plate that will be used for years to come. You can transform an inexpensive clear glass plate by decoupaging on motifs cut from wrapping paper or greeting cards. Sponge background paints on; then seal the plate with an aerosol acrylic.

MATERIALS
❋ Clear glass plate
❋ High-quality wrapping paper or greeting cards with desired motifs
❋ Scissors with fine, sharp blades and points
❋ Decoupage medium; brush or sponge applicator
❋ Sponge or brayer
❋ Acrylic paints
❋ Small piece of natural sea sponge for applying paints
❋ Aerosol acrylic paint (optional)
❋ Aerosol clear acrylic sealer
❋ Miscellaneous items: glass cleaner, lint-free rags, newspaper

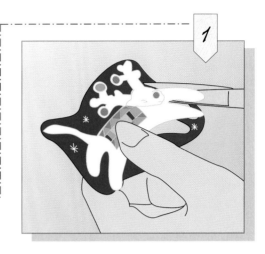

1 Cut desired motifs from wrapping paper. If heavy paper, such as a greeting card, is used, reduce the thickness by peeling away one or more layers of paper. Cut any intricate motifs from paper by first cutting a smooth curve around design. Cut details by holding scissors stationary and moving motif. Use curved cuticle scissors to cut out very fine details. Cut with points of blades away from motif.

2 Trace the plate on piece of paper; plan placement of motifs. Clean back of plate thoroughly, using glass cleaner and lint-free rag. Place plate facedown on newspaper on table.

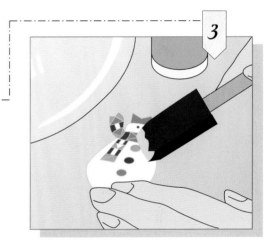

3 Apply a thin layer of decoupage medium to front of foreground motif, using sponge applicator, brush or finger. Position motif on back of plate; smooth out with dampened sponge or brayer. Excess decoupage medium around edges of motif will not show when plate is painted.

4 Continue applying motifs as desired, working from foreground to background if motifs are layered. Allow to dry. Apply thin coat of decoupage medium to back of motifs as a sealer; allow to dry.

5 Apply lightest color of acrylic paint to back of plate, using sea sponge; apply sparingly. Allow to dry. Apply the remaining layers of paint, finishing with the darkest color. If desired, paint back of plate a solid color, using aerosol acrylic paint. Allow to dry.

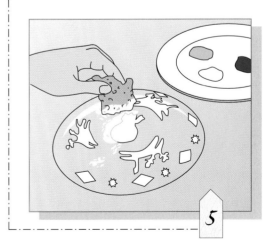

6 Personalize plate on back with your signature and the date, using permanent-ink marking pen. Mark where signature won't show through front of plate, if back of plate is not painted a solid color. Apply light coat of aerosol acrylic sealer; allow to dry. Apply second coat.

7 Decoupaged plates are not dishwasher safe, and should be washed by hand with the barest minimum of soaking time in the sink.

PLANT COVER-UPS

Deck the hall with boughs of holly and adorn houseplants with Christmas trees and gingerbread boys! Here is the perfect gift for that plant lover you know, or to put on the poinsettia you bring to a holiday party. The greenery will abound with the spirit of Christmas when these colorful plastic canvas cover-ups are tied on.

MATERIALS

For Each Cover-up
* 7-mesh clear plastic canvas, 1/4 sheet
* No. 16 tapestry needle

For the Tree
* Worsted weight yarn: green, 10 yd. (9.15 m); white, red, gold metallic, 1 yd. (0.95 m) each
* Ivory ruffled lace trim, 5/8" (1.5 cm) wide, 5" (12.5 cm)

* Green satin ribbon, 3/8" (1 cm), 2/3 yd. (0.63 m)
* Hot glue gun or white craft glue

For the Gingerbread Boy
* Worsted weight yarn: tan, 8 yd. (7.35 m); white, 3 yd. (2.75 m); black, 2 yd. (1.85 m); red, 1 yd. (0.95 m)
* Satin ribbon: 3/8" (1 cm) red, 2/3 yd. (0.63 m); 1/8" (3 mm) green, 1/4 yd. (0.25 m)
* Miscellaneous items: scissors, ruler

1 Follow the bold outline on the Charts to cut each design. Cut up to, but not into, the edge bars. Refer to page 156 for Plastic Canvas Instructions and Stitches.

2 **Tree:** Work the star with gold continental stitches, then overcast the star edge. Work the tree with the leaf stitch and green yarn. For the ornaments, work alternating red and white French knots on branches.

3 Overcast the tree edges with green yarn. Glue the lace to the bottom edge of the tree on the wrong side.

4 **Gingerbread Boy:** Cross-stitch the hearts and nose with red and work the body with tan and white continental stitches. Using black yarn, make French knots for the eyes and backstitch the mouth.

5 Use red yarn to work varying length Gobelin stitches for the background. Separate two plies of black yarn and backstitch around the outline of the gingerbread boy. Overcast outer edges with red yarn.

6 Thread the tapestry needle with the ⅛" (3 mm) green ribbon. Thread ribbon through dots at neck, front to back, and tie the ends into a bow.

Ribbon Ties: Cut the ⅜" (1 cm) ribbon in half and knot one end. Use the red ribbon for the gingerbread boy and the green ribbon for the tree. Thread the
7 opposite end through the tapestry needle and insert through back where marked on Chart with arrows. Pull ribbon through until caught by knot. Repeat for the other side. Tie ribbon around plant pot.

COLOR/STITCH KEY	
symbol	color/stitch
Gingerbread Boy	
/	Red Gobelin
∘	Tan
×	Red Cross-stitch
•	White
Tree	
•	Red French Knot
∘	White French Knot
/	Green
♪	Metallic Gold

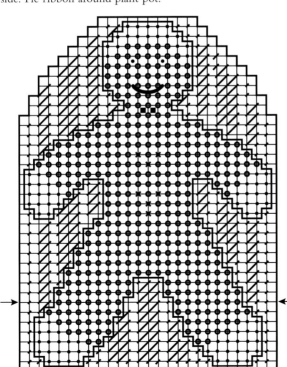

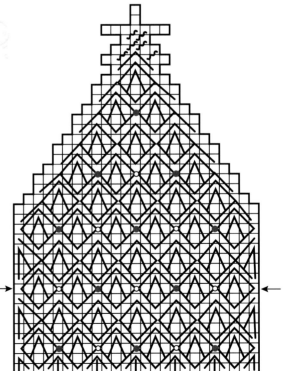

PINECONE KINDLERS

For an inexpensive gift that is both useful and decorative, fill a basket with pinecone kindlers. Pinecones are dipped in melted paraffin wax and cooled in muffin cups. Candlewicks keep the pinecones burning for up to twenty minutes, while kindling logs for the fire. Paraffin for the kindlers can be colored red and scented with cinnamon, or colored green and scented with pine, if desired. To light a fire, center a pinecone kindler under stacked firewood and light the wick.

MATERIALS
❋ Double boiler
❋ Paraffin wax, approximately 1 lb. (450 g) per six pinecones
❋ Candle color squares and candle scent squares, one square each per lb. (450 g) of paraffin wax
❋ Candy thermometer
❋ Muffin tin
❋ Nonstick vegetable oil spray
❋ Wax-coated candlewicks, 6″ (15 cm) long
❋ Pinecones, 2″ (5 cm) in diameter or size to fit muffin cups
❋ Miscellaneous items: scissors, wooden spoon, paper towels, tongs

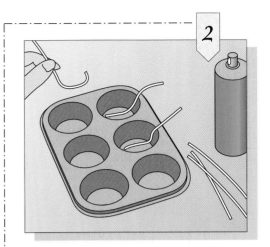

1 Insert candy thermometer into double boiler. Melt 1 lb. (450 g) paraffin wax in top of double boiler over boiling water. Add one square of the candle color and one square of candle scent as desired. Mix gently, using wooden spoon.

2 Spray the muffin cups lightly with nonstick vegetable oil spray. Place one end of wax-coated candlewick in each muffin cup; allow opposite end to hang over side of muffin cup. — · — · — · —

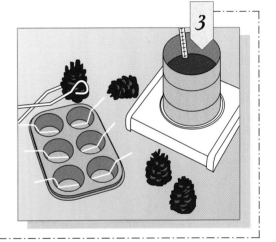

3 Cool melted paraffin to about 160°F/70°C. Dip pinecone in paraffin, turning to coat thoroughly. Raise pinecone above wax for a few seconds, allowing paraffin to harden; repeat two or three times. Remove with tongs, and place coated pinecone upright in muffin cup over candlewick. — · — · — · —

4 Remove top pan of double boiler containing remaining melted paraffin. Dry outside of pan with towel to prevent water from dripping into muffin cups. Slowly pour ½" (1.3 cm) melted paraffin into each muffin cup at base of pinecone. — · — · — · —

5 Allow the kindlers to cool completely. Remove from muffin cups. Arrange in decorative gift basket; prepare note card with instructions for use.

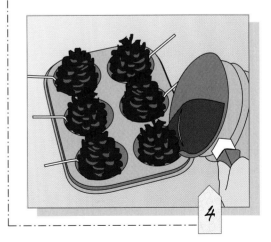

APPLE CHECKERBOARD

Take time during the busy holiday season to play—on a checkerboard you made yourself! Using purchased apples, blocks and a plaque, the only woodworking you need to do is drill a few holes and saw a dowel into pieces. A perfect beginner's project, hone up on your checker-playing skills right up until you wrap this up for the game-lover in your family.

MATERIALS

❋ 9" x 12" (23 x 30.5 cm) basswood plaque (See Sources on page 160 for purchasing information)
❋ ³/₄" (2 cm) wood blocks, 24
❋ ¹/₂" (1.3 cm) wood apples, 12
❋ ¹/₈" (3 mm) wood dowel, 8" (20.5 cm)
❋ Mediumweight jute, ¹/₃ yd. (0.32 m)
❋ Checkered stencil with 1" (2.5 cm) squares
❋ Acrylic paints: green, red

❋ Stencil paint creme, brown
❋ Fruitwood gel wood stain
❋ Waterbase varnish
❋ Paintbrushes: stencil, ³/₄" (2 cm) flat
❋ Tools: electric drill with ¹/₈" and ⁵/₃₂" drill bits, saw, pliers
❋ Glues: stencil adhesive, thick white craft glue
❋ Miscellaneous items: ruler, pencil, paper towels, fine sandpaper, tack cloth

Gameboard: Lightly draw a line 1½" (3.8 cm) from each end. On each line,
measure 1⅝" (4 cm) from each side and mark six dots, 1¼" (3.2 cm) apart. Drill
½" (1.3 cm) deep holes at each dot using the ⁵⁄₃₂" bit.

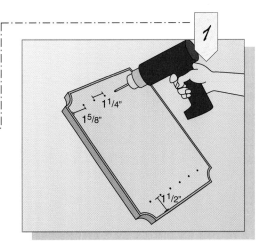

2 Erase lines on board, and sand to smooth. Wipe with tack cloth. Using
paper towels, evenly apply the gel wood stain to all surfaces, following
direction of grain. Let dry.

3 Follow manufacturer's instructions to apply stencil adhesive to stencil back.
Refer to the photo to position the stencil on gameboard. Use stencil brush and
stencil creme to paint the pattern. Let dry overnight.

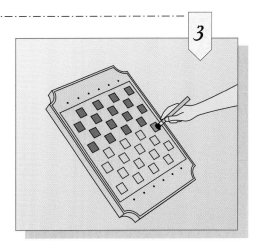

4 **Blocks:** On one side of each wood block, mark a center dot. Drill ½"
(1.3 cm) deep holes at each dot using the ⁵⁄₃₂" bit.

5 **Apples:** Use the ⅛" drill bit to drill ⅛" (3 mm) deep holes in the bottom of
each apple. Hold the apples with pliers while drilling. Cut twelve ⅝" (1.5 cm)
pieces from dowel. Insert and glue a dowel in each hole.

6 **Painting:** Use the flat brush to paint 6 apples and 12 blocks green. Paint
the remaining blocks and apples red. **Do not paint drilled side of the
blocks.** Let dry.

7 **Finishing:** Lightly sand the blocks, especially corners and edges, to achieve an
antiqued look. Wipe with tack cloth. Use paper towels to apply gel wood stain
to all surfaces of apples and blocks. Let dry.

8 Glue a small jute piece into each apple top for stem. Use brush to apply
two to three coats of varnish to all pieces. Let dry between coats.

9 **Playing:** To play, refer to the photo to insert apples in holes and arrange blocks
on gameboard. To crown an opponent's piece, turn over the block and insert a
matching colored apple.

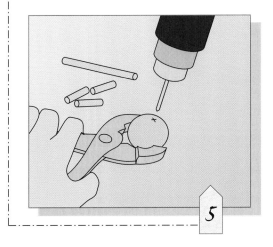

Have a cookie exchange party and ask all guests to bring a designated number of cookies to swap as well as recipes. The fun will begin as everyone samples the assortment of cookies and fills the cookie bags you whipped up with delicious goodies to take home. Our charming version of Rudolph is appliquéd onto the cookie bags. Made of brown pin-dot fabric, he wears a scarf and bell and, of course, sports a bright red nose.

MATERIALS

For Each Reindeer Appliqué
※ Cotton fabric: brown pin-dot, 5″ x 6″ (12.5 cm x 15 cm); red pin-dot, 1¹/₂″ x 3″ (3.8 x 7.5 cm); red/white stripe, 2¹/₂″ x 3″ (6.5 x 7.5 cm)
※ Lightweight fusible interfacing, 5″ x 6″ (12.5 x 15 cm)
※ Fusible web, 9″ x 12″ (23 x 30.5 cm)
※ ¹/₈″ (3 mm) green satin ribbon, 6″ (15 cm)
※ Dimensional fabric paints: black, red, white
※ ¹/₄″ (6 mm) gold bell
※ 5 mm red pom-pom

For Each Cookie Bag
※ Cotton fabric, stripe or small print, 9¹/₂″ x 13″ (24.3 x 33 cm)

※ 1″ (2.5 cm) white ruffled eyelet, ³/₈ yd. (0.35 m)
※ ¹/₁₆″ (1.5 mm) white satin ribbon, ³/₈ yd. (0.35 m)
※ Assorted ribbons and trims, your choice, ¹/₂ yd. (0.5 m) each
※ ³/₄″ (2 cm) decorative Christmas button
※ Large-eyed embroidery needle
※ Pattern sheet
※ Miscellaneous items: white craft glue, tracing paper, pencil, scissors, sewing machine, matching sewing threads, iron, straight pins, plastic bag with sealable closure

1 **Reindeer Appliqué:** Iron the interfacing onto the wrong side of the brown pin-dot fabric and fusible web to the wrong side of each fabric piece. Trace the four patterns onto tracing paper and cut from appropriate fabrics. Dashed lines on patterns represent overlapped areas.

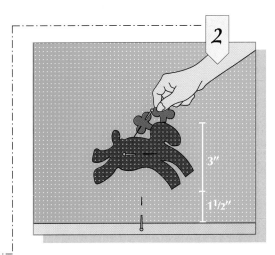

2 **Placement:** Fold fabric in half with 9½" (24.3 cm) edges together, and pin-mark center front at top and bottom of fabric. Place fabric flat, right side up. See illustration to center reindeer along center-front line, about 1½" (3.8 cm) from bottom edge; pin. Tuck antlers under top of head; pin.

3 **Appliquéing:** Fuse antlers, then reindeer body. Use a narrow zigzag stitch and matching thread to machine-appliqué edges. Repeat for ears and scarf.

4 **Embellishing:** Use dimensional paints to paint the eyes black and mouth red; let dry. Add white highlight on each eye. Sew bell below neck. Make a small bow from ⅛" (3 mm) green satin ribbon. Glue bow above bell and pom-pom to nose with craft glue.

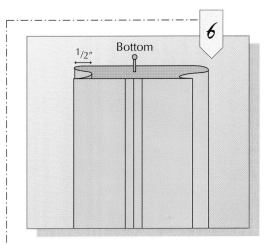

5 **Cookie Bag:** Pin eyelet to right side of fabric along top 13" (33 cm) edge, matching raw edges. Stitch ¼" (6 mm) seam and press eyelet up. Sew any additional ribbon and trims along top edge, if desired.

6 Pin 9½" (24.3 cm) edges, right sides together, and sew a ¼" (6 mm) seam. See illustration and, with right side in, place seam over center foldline and pin. Pin ½" (1.3 cm) side pleats along bottom, as shown. Stitch ¼" (6 mm) seam across bottom, and turn right side out.

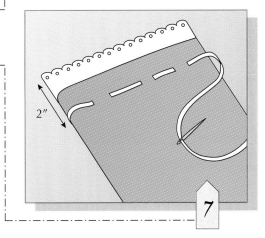

7 **Bag Drawstring:** Thread white 1/16" (1.5 mm) ribbon in needle. Beginning 2" (5 cm) below top of eyelet, sew a running stitch on right side around bag.

8 **Finishing:** Using varying widths and colors of ribbon, make a multiloop bow and sew to top right edge of bag. Sew button to center of bow. Insert plastic bag inside cookie bag for liner.

MILLEFIORI BEAD NECKLACE

Everyone on your gift list will love a necklace strung with handmade beads! Create the beads on this festive necklace in a snap with Millefiori clay canes! Just roll balls of clay, then cover them with slices of a cane. So quick and easy to make, it's a perfect gift for a teacher, your secret pal or the babysitter.

MATERIALS
* Oven bake clay: white, green; 1/4 block of each
* Millefiori clay canes: zinnia, candy cane; one each
* Beads: 6 mm emerald round, 24; 14 mm gold disc, 12
* Thin metallic gold cord, 1 yd. (0.95 m)
* Clay warmer (optional)
* Miscellaneous items: sharp single-edge razor blade, needle tool or awl, seven round toothpicks, metal baking pan, two wood skewers, oven, ruler

1 **Beads:** Warm the clay in your hands or in a clay warmer. Knead the green and white clays separately until soft and pliable. Roll four green and three white clay balls, each ⅜" (1 cm) in diameter. Keep the clay balls warm until ready to use.

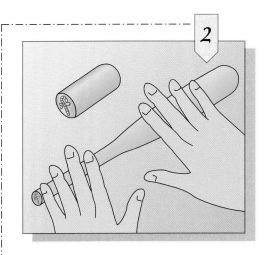

2 **Decorative Cane:** Each cane must be worked until it is only ⅜" (1 cm) in diameter. Warm each cane between your palms or in a clay warmer. Starting in the middle of the cane, gently squeeze or press while rotating to compress and lengthen it. Then roll the cane between your palms. Or, pinch and roll the cane to reduce the diameter. With either method, work slowly and be sure the cane is warm or it may shatter. Cut off the distorted ends of the cane with the razor blade. ─ · ─ · ─ · ─ ·

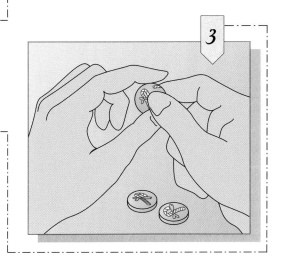

3 **Covering Beads:** Use a sharp razor blade to cut 13 to 15 slices from each cane. They will look like those in the photo, except smaller. Cover the surface of the green beads with candy cane slices and the white beads with zinnia slices. Press each bead with your fingers to smooth the seams. Then roll it between your palms until smooth and round. ─ · ─ · ─ · ─ · ─ ·

4 **Bead Holes:** Use the needle tool or awl to pierce completely through the center of the bead from one side. Remove the tool and insert it through the bead from the other side. With the needle tool through bead, roll the bead on your palm to enlarge the hole. Remove the needle tool and insert a toothpick through the bead hole for baking.

5 **Baking:** Position skewers 1¼" (3.2 cm) apart across the metal baking pan with the skewer ends resting on pan sides. Suspend the beads on the skewers by toothpick ends. Follow manufacturer's instructions for temperatures and baking times. Beads in this project were baked in a preheated 265°F/130°C oven for 30 minutes, and allowed to cool in the oven. ─ · ─ · ─ · ─ · ─ · ─ ·

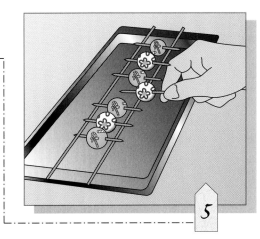

6 **Stringing:** Refer to the photo to string beads on the gold cord with 1½" (3.8 cm) between beaded sections, tying a knot at the beginning and end of each section. Knot cord ends to adjust to desired length; trim the ends if necessary.

BUTTON DOLLS

As an ornament for the Christmas tree, or perfectly poised on a desk at work, each 5" (12.5 cm) miss is cute as a button. Part of the fun of crafting her is picking out the many colorful buttons that make her arms and legs. A single scallop from a crocheted doily makes her collar, and peeking below her dress are pantaloons!

MATERIALS

* Wood shapes: 2¹/₂" (6.5 cm) doll form; ¹/₂" (1.3 cm) spools, two
* Buttons, assorted coordinating colors: ¹/₄" to ³/₈" (6 mm to 1 cm) for arms, nine matching pairs; ¹/₂" to ⁵/₈" (1.3 to 1.5 cm) for legs, 15 matching pairs
* Miniprint cotton fabric, your choice, 4" x 10" (10 x 25.5 cm)
* 4" (10 cm) round white crocheted doily with scallops
* 1¹/₂" (3.8 cm) white flat lace, ¹/₃ yd. (0.32 m)
* Mini-curl doll hair, your color choice
* 2" (5 cm) sinamay hat, coordinating color
* Mini ribbon rose, coordinating color
* ¹/₈" (3 mm) green satin ribbon, 1" (2.5 cm)
* Metallic cord for hanger, 6" (15 cm)
* Acrylic paints: apricot, clay, rose, black, color to coordinate with fabric
* Paintbrushes: No. 10 flat, fine spotter, small round fabric
* Hot glue gun
* Miscellaneous items: disposable palette, scissors, ruler, wax dental floss, spray starch, iron, sewing needle and matching thread, sewing machine

---

Painting: Refer to page 158 for Painting Instructions and Techniques. Refer to photo for all steps below. Basecoat doll form with two coats of apricot. Paint a small nose with spotter brush and clay paint. Dip the brush handle in black paint to dot eyes. Using the fabric brush, lightly blush cheeks with rose. Paint center of each spool desired color, leaving top and bottom unpainted.

1

2 **Legs:** Place 14 matching pairs of buttons in two vertical rows with two slightly larger ones at bottom for feet. Also select one ⅝" (1.5 cm) button for center point of the legs. Cut 12" (30.5 cm) of dental floss. Lace floss end through two holes on one foot; knot twice. String, in ascending order, six buttons in first row, one spool, then seven buttons. Lace floss through two holes of the ⅝" (1.5 cm) center button. String the second button row in descending order, seven buttons, one spool, then six buttons.

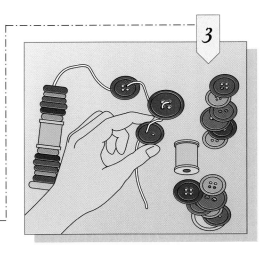

3 Lace floss through two holes of button foot. Loosely space buttons on floss to measure 5" (12.5 cm); knot twice at foot. Dot each knot with hot glue; trim ends. Squeeze glue between each foot and adjacent button.

4 **Arms:** Place nine matching pairs of buttons in two vertical rows with two slightly larger ones at bottom for hands. Cut 12" (30.5 cm) of dental floss. Lace floss end through two holes on one hand; knot twice. String the first button row in ascending order, then second row in descending order. Repeat Step 3 for arms, loosely spacing buttons to measure 4½" (11.5 cm).

5 **Dress:** Press fabric in half lengthwise with wrong sides together. Sew gathering stitches ¼" (6 mm) from long raw edges, leaving 3" (7.5 cm) threads at each end.

6 **Collar and Pantaloons:** Spray doily with starch, and iron. See the illustration to cut one scallop in a pie-shape wedge from doily; slit as indicated. For the pantaloons, starting at body back, glue lace twice around doll to hang ½" (1.3 cm) below body.

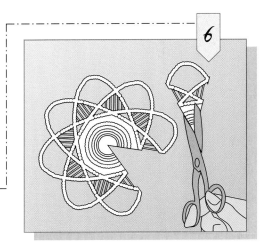

7 **Assembly:** Hot-glue large center button of legs to doll bottom, making sure legs hang evenly. Glue inner row of lace to center button between legs for pantaloons. Gather dress, and tie around neck with ends at center back; knot ends, and trim. Adjust gathers, and glue back seam. Spot-glue inside dress to upper body. Wrap collar around neck with scallop at front; overlap and glue ends. Spot-glue collar to dress front. With even number of arm buttons positioned on each side, center and glue floss around back of neck.

8 **Finishing:** Wrap a double strand of doll hair around hand approximately 40 times. Holding hair between forefinger and thumb, cut at opposite side. Twist hair at center. Hot-glue top, side and back of head; press hair in glue just above forehead, stretching curls in glue on sides and back; trim as desired.

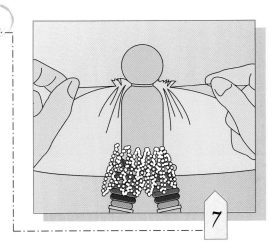

9 Hot-glue hat on head. Turn brim up, and spot-glue. Glue green satin ribbon for leaves and mini ribbon rose to center front brim. Trim leaves at an angle. For the hanger, thread cord through center hat crown; knot.

SNOWFLAKE SWEATSHIRT

You'll look smashing at your next holiday gathering dressed in a snowflake sweatshirt. Beautiful Battenberg doilies duplicate the look and feel of huge white snowflakes on this designer-look sweatshirt. A touch of sparkle from glitter and jewels adds an air of holiday excitement. It's versatile enough to wear shopping and stunning enough to don for a party.

MATERIALS

❋ Red sweatshirt, prewashed
❋ 1½" (3.8 cm) red/green grosgrain ribbon, 1⅓ yd. (1.27 m)
❋ Red sequin string, 1⅓ yd. (1.27 m)
❋ White Battenberg doilies: 6" (15 cm), three; 12" (30.5 cm), one
❋ 45" (115 cm) cotton poinsettia print fabric, with 4" (10 cm) diameter poinsettias, ¼ yd. (0.25 m)
❋ Fusible interfacing, ⅛ yd. (0.15 m)
❋ 4 mm crystal faceted flatback acrylic jewels, 15
❋ Fabric glue
❋ Red glitter paint
❋ T-shirt board
❋ Miscellaneous items: wax paper, damp sponge, scissors, iron

1 Place sweatshirt over T-shirt board. Cut ribbon and sequin string in half. Cut a V in one end of each ribbon.

2 Cut a square of fabric around three poinsettias. Cut three squares of interfacing to match fabric squares. Fuse interfacing onto wrong side of each fabric square. Cut around poinsettia and leaves in detail.

3 Place 12" (30.5 cm) doily right side down on a sheet of wax paper, and spread glue evenly to completely cover back of doily. Wipe fingers on dampened sponge. Place doily on center shirt front, and press firmly in place.

4 Use a new piece of wax paper for each following gluing step. Apply glue to reverse side of each ribbon. Press onto shirt beginning at each shoulder, making an X and crossing on center front. Repeat to glue sequins, pressing into place down center of each ribbon.

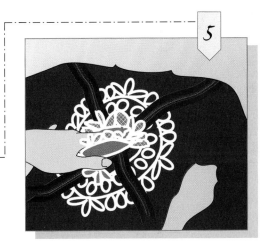

5 Glue one 6" (15 cm) doily over center front at ribbon/sequin crossover and one over ribbon/sequin ends at each shoulder.

6 Cover back of poinsettias with glue and press one firmly over center of each 6" (15 cm) doily.

7 When glue is dry, remove shirt from board and turn shirt inside out. Press on wrong side with warm iron to strengthen glue bond.

8 Place shirt on board again, and apply a line of red glitter paint around cut edges of poinsettia, with glitter line half on fabric and half on doily.

9 Place a drop of glitter on back of each jewel and press five into a cluster on the center of each poinsettia. Let glitter dry completely before washing.

10 Turn shirt to inside, and wash by hand or on gentle cycle in cool water. Line dry.

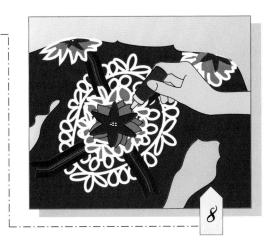

WINTER VEST

snow-flakes, Polar bears, What Santa might bring Winter is always my favorite thing

Celebrate the joy of the holidays and the splendor of fresh-fallen snow with this whimsical winter vest. Screen-paint and appliqué a 3-dimensional polar bear on the vest front. Finish by painting a smattering of snowflakes and a simple verse declaring just a few of the things that make the season so special.

MATERIALS

❋ Stonewash blue felt vest
❋ 9" x 12" (23 x 30.5 cm) white felt square
❋ Blank paint screen
❋ Paint-screen holder
❋ Paint-screen fabric paints: white, gold, burgundy, gray, light green, black, dark green
❋ Embroidery floss: ecru, light gray
❋ Polyester fiberfill
❋ Pattern sheet
❋ Miscellaneous items: tracing paper, pencil, large-eyed sewing needle, scissors

1   Use six strands of ecru floss to work blanket stitches around all the edges of vest. See the Step 1 illustration and page 157 Embroidery Stitches for how to do the blanket stitch.

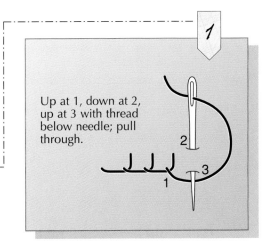

Up at 1, down at 2, up at 3 with thread below needle; pull through.

2   Trace the pattern onto blank paint screen with pencil, following any manufacturer's instructions. Center pattern onto white felt and insert in paint-screen holder.

3   Follow manufacturer's instructions to squeeze paint through screen pattern and screen-paint polar bear and mouse. Use black for outlines, gray for mouse, dark green for holly leaves, and burgundy for bow, hat and candy cane stripes. Let dry. Cut out the design, leaving ¼" (6 mm) border on all sides.

4   Referring to the photo for placement, screen-paint trees and snow on vest. Use light green for trees, gold for stars, black for snow outline and white for snow. Let dry.

5   Refer to the pattern to position polar bear between trees. See the Step 5 illustration and page 157 Embroidery Stitches to sew polar bear to vest using running stitches and three strands of light gray floss.

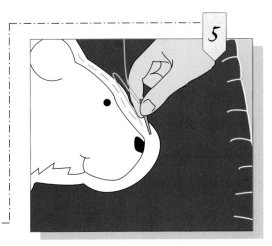

6   Carefully cut a 2" (5 cm) slit on inside of vest only at center of polar bear. Stuff with fiberfill. Slipstitch opening closed.

7   To paint the right side of the vest, use white and refer to the photo to screen-paint the following words: Snowflakes, Polar bears, What Santa might bring, Winter is always my favorite thing. Dot each "i" with an asterisk snowflake.

8   To finish the left side of the vest, use white to screen-paint scattered asterisks and dot snowflakes above the polar bear.

JEWELED TREE SHIRT

You'll love trimming this shirt almost as much as you'll love receiving the compliments on your handiwork. It's as easy as 1-2-3! Shop for the jewels at your local craft store, use chalk to mark the placement, and glue the garland chain and gems for a dazzling design.

MATERIALS

❋ Green cotton-blend sweatshirt
❋ T-shirt board
❋ Gold-link chain, 50" (127 cm)
❋ Acrylic round stones: 25 mm, one; 18 mm, three; 11 mm, 10; 7 mm, 26
❋ Acrylic square stones: 17 mm, four; 12 mm, two
❋ Acrylic 18 mm oval stones, two
❋ Acrylic 15 mm stars, 12
❋ Acrylic 13 mm triangles, six
❋ Acrylic hearts: 18 mm, two; 11 x 10 mm, yellow, 21

❋ Acrylic pear shapes, 18 x 8 mm, six
❋ Acrylic navette stones, 17 x 7 mm, 22
❋ Acrylic mirrors: 13 mm round, 28 mm round, 18 mm square; two each
❋ Bugle beads, 1" (2.5 cm), 21 for candles
❋ Glues: jewelry, industrial-grade adhesive
❋ Miscellaneous items: wire cutters, toothpicks, chalk

Placement Guide

Follow this guide
to center tree on shirt
front. Mark dots
at 2" intervals.

2" — Bugle Bead Candle

— Chain

2"

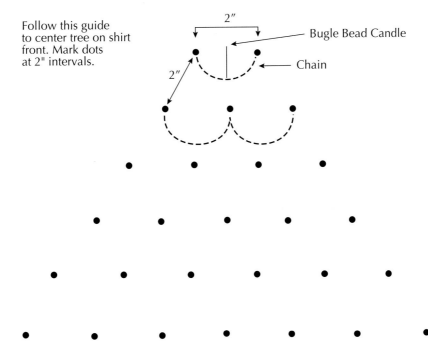

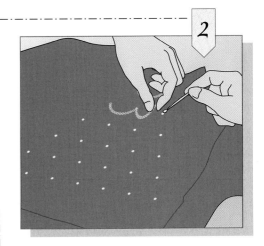

1 **Preparation:** Insert T-board in sweatshirt. Refer to the Placement Guide to draw chalk dots centered on shirt front for tree design.

2 **Chain:** Cut into 3" (7.5 cm), 5" (12.5 cm), 7½" (19.3 cm), 11" (28 cm), 14" (35.5 cm), and 16" (40.5 cm) lengths. Beginning at top of design, apply small dot of industrial-grade adhesive with toothpick to the top two chalk dots. Drape the 3" (7.5 cm) chain between glue dots. Continue gluing and draping each successive length of chain between horizontal rows of dots.

3 **Bugle Bead Candles:** Apply a vertical line of adhesive with toothpick beginning at center bottom of each chain drape. Carefully place bead onto glue line. Let dry thoroughly. Glue an upside-down heart to top of each candle for a flame.

4 **Acrylic Stones:** Refer to the photo to lay out design, beginning with largest stones, then smaller ones. To glue each stone to shirt, apply a dot of jewelry glue on shirt and on center back of each stone.

5 **Star:** Attach one 18 mm oval stone at tree top, leaving room to glue five triangle stones around it.

6 **Tree Base:** Glue the two 18 mm square mirrors horizontally together, with 25 mm round stone centered above and a 12 mm square stone on each side.

POP-UP CARDS

These elegant pop-up cards require no special talents—even a child can make them. Marbled, green and red papers; gold foil; glue; a marking pen; scalloping shears; scissors and a paper punch are the only supplies you will need to craft exquisite cards and envelopes in half the time it would take to paint and draw. Then use the time you save to write a long letter to dear friends.

MATERIALS

For Each Card

✳ Marbled paper, 11" x 14" (28 x 35.5 cm) sheet
✳ Green paper, 11" x 14" (28 x 35.5 cm) sheet for tree card
✳ Red paper, 8" x 11" (20.5 cm x 28 cm) sheet for angel card
✳ Double-faced gold foil, 8" x 11" (20.5 cm x 28 cm) sheet
✳ White craft glue
✳ Gold metallic marking pen
✳ Scalloping shears, or other decorative edge scissors
✳ Pattern sheet
✳ Miscellaneous items: pencil, tracing paper, scissors, paper punch

Either Card: Cut marbled paper in half, making two 7" x 11" (18 x 28 cm) pieces, one for card and one for envelope. Cut card marbled paper and gold foil to measure 9¼" x 6½" (23.6 x 16.3 cm). Glue foil to back of marbled paper, spreading a narrow band of glue along edges. Fold card in half with foil inside. Cut front edges of card with scalloping shears to reveal foil along edges when card is closed. — — — — — — — —

1

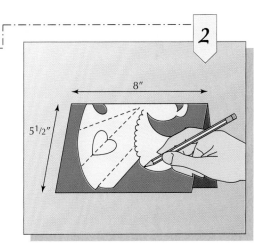

Angel Card: Trace angel pattern and cut out. Fold red paper in half; place center foldline on fold, and trace around pattern. Cut out angel, center foldline heart and halo. Open angel, and fanfold skirt. Using cutout heart as pattern, trace and cut out hearts on skirt side panels. — · — · — ·

2

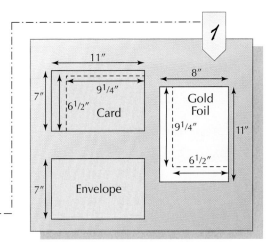

Cut bottom edge of skirt and wings with scalloping shears. Punch holes along bottom edge of skirt with paper punch. Draw around hearts and scalloped edges and fill in halo with gold metallic marking pen. Fold skirt tabs to inside. Position folded angel inside foil card; glue tabs to card.

3

Tree Card: Trace tree and star patterns, and cut out. Fold green paper in half; place pattern center foldline on fold, and trace around pattern. Cut out tree, and curve cutouts on center fold. Open tree, and fanfold. Trace branch cutouts on folded edges and cut out each section, one at a time.

4

Draw gold lines along branch edges with gold metallic pen. Glue star to tree top, creasing center to match center fold of tree. Punch out foil dots, and glue randomly on tree. Fold tree, and place inside foil card. Mark where bottom corners of tree touch card; glue corners only to card.

5

Envelope: See the illustration to fold marbled paper. Place a line of glue along side edges below fold. Fold up and glue along center side edges. Cut a 1" (2.5 cm) strip of foil the width of top edge of envelope. Glue it to top back edge, extending foil ¼" (6 mm). Trim with scalloping shears. — · — · — ·

6

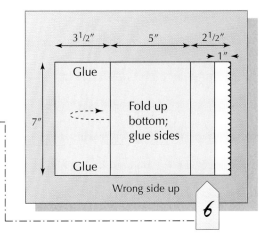

*C*reate personalized holiday greetings by making your own embossed cards and gift tags. The embossed, or raised, design is made by placing paper over a stencil cutout and rubbing along the design with a stylus, a hard-pointed, pen-shaped tool. To add sparkle to the card, highlight the embossed design with glitter. Designs for stencils can be found on Christmas cards or in stencil design books. Or for super-easy cards, buy precut stencils, found in most craft stores.

MATERIALS
❋ Card-stock or heavyweight stationery
❋ Transparent Mylar® sheets
❋ Fine-point permanent-ink marking pen
❋ Paper cutter; or mat knife, cutting surface, such as a cutting mat, and metal straightedge
❋ Stylus or small plastic crochet hook, for tracing design
❋ Removable transparent tape
❋ Glue pen, extra-fine glitter, and soft artist's eraser, for glittered cards
❋ Light box or other illuminated glass surface
❋ Cording, for gift tag
❋ Miscellaneous items: scissors, hole punch

1   To make your own stencil, position Mylar over design, allowing a 1" (2.5 cm) border; secure with tape. Trace design, using permanent-ink marking pen; simplify the shapes as necessary.

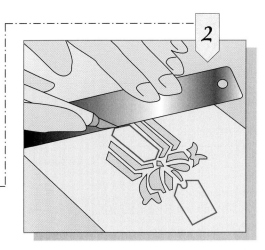

2   Cut out inner details of the design, using mat knife; use straightedge to cut along the straight lines. Cut and remove the smallest areas first, then larger ones. Pull knife toward you as you cut; turn Mylar, rather than knife, to change directions.

3   Redraw outer lines of design as necessary, to touch up any lines that were removed when cutting. Cut excess Mylar from outer edges of the design, using a mat knife and a straightedge; leave at least ¼" (6 mm) border.

4   If you are cutting your own cards and tags, cut and fold the paper to the finished size before embossing. If a paper cutter is not available, use a metal straightedge, a mat knife, and a cutting mat. Use card-stock or heavyweight stationery to prevent any tearing during embossing. Most print shops have paper, cards, and envelopes in a variety of weights and colors. Position the stencil as desired on front of card; secure stencil with removable tape.

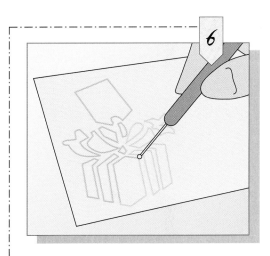

5   Place a small lamp under a glass-top table if a light box is unavailable. Tape a piece of tracing paper over the glass to act as a light diffuser, if necessary.

6   Place the card, stencil side down, on light table. Using stylus, trace outline of the design, applying firm pressure. Retrace, if necessary, for clear definition. Trace around outer edges of stencil, if desired, to frame the design. If the stylus has two ball ends, use the large end of the stylus for tracing large design areas and the small end for fine details. If the stylus squeaks as it is moved across the paper, lubricate the end by rubbing it in the palm of your hand.

7   Remove stencil. For glittered cards, apply glue to desired design details; sprinkle glitter over the wet glue. Shake off the excess glitter; allow glue to dry. Remove any excess glitter from card, using soft artist's eraser. Personalize card with initials, using a permanent-ink marking pen.

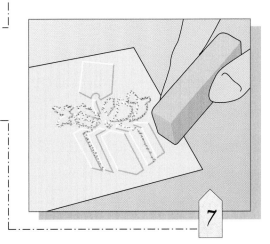

8   Punch hole in upper left corner of card to make gift tag. Cut 8" (20.5 cm) length of cording. Fold cording in half, and insert folded end through tag; bring the cut ends through the loop, and pull to secure.

GIFT BAGS & TAGS

The gift bag is a favorite way to wrap holiday packages, though the high cost of some store-bought bags can break your budget in a hurry. But a crafter can decorate her own for a fraction of the cost! A plain brown bag becomes a cute gift sack with simple fabric cutouts and a few embellishments. Knowing the one-of-a-kind bag was handmade with love, its recipient will take even more pleasure in finding what's inside!

MATERIALS

* 8" x 10¼" (20.5 x 26.1 cm) brown bag with handles
* Brown paper grocery bag
* Double-sided sheet adhesive
* Red raffia
* Medium-point black permanent marker
* Hot glue gun

For the Snowman Bag

* Miniprint cotton fabrics: white, 4" x 7" (10 x 18 cm); burgundy, 3" x 3" (7.5 x 7.5 cm); gold, black, blue plaid, 2" x 3" (5 x 7.5 cm) each
* 2½" (6.5 cm) cinnamon stick, one

* Natural raffia
* Jute, 10" (25.5 cm)
* Trims: ½" (1.3 cm) green flat button; yellow split pea, one each; red beans, two

For the Star Bag

* Miniprint cotton fabrics: gold, 6" x 7" (15 x 18 cm); red check, green check, small amount of each for patches
* ½" (1.3 cm) burgundy flat buttons, five
* Pattern sheet
* Miscellaneous items: tracing paper, pencil, scissors, hole punch

Patterns: Follow the manufacturer's instructions to adhere sheet adhesive to the back of each fabric. Trace the patterns and cut out. For the star bag, cut out three star patterns, and cut fabric as directed for a total of four stars. Also cut three ¼" to ½" (6 mm to 1.3 cm) patches from the red and green check fabrics. For the snowman bag, cut out the remaining seven pattern pieces, and cut fabrics as directed.

1

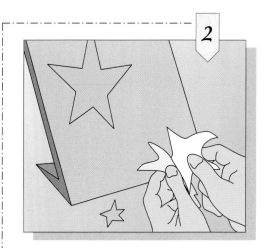

Fabric Cutouts: Cut a 2¼" x 4" (6 x 10 cm) strip from the brown paper grocery bag. Fold it in half to make a 2" x 2¼" (5 x 6 cm) tag. Punch a hole in the upper left corner of the tag for hanging. Refer to the photo to position and adhere the fabric cutouts to the front of the bags and gift tags.

2

Star Bag: Refer to the photo to glue the buttons to the bag front and on the large star. Use the black marker to draw pen-stitch lines around each star, mock stitches on each patch, and lines and dashes around the edges of the bag.

3

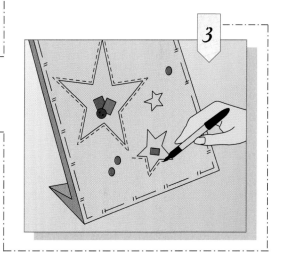

Snowman Bag: Glue the green button to the snowman's scarf, the split pea to the center of the face for a nose, and the red beans to the body for buttons. Cut the jute in half, and tie two small bows. Glue a bow on each boot.

4

Cut ten 4" (10 cm) lengths of natural raffia for the broom; set aside one length. Align the raffia ends, fold in half and tie to the bottom of the cinnamon stick with the remaining raffia length. Glue broom to the snowman's mitten. Use the black marker to draw arms, eyes and mouth on the snowman and lines and stars around the edges of the bag.

5

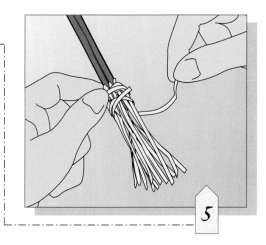

Gift Tags: Use red raffia to tie the gift tag to the front handle of the bag, and a bow above the tag. Use the black marker to draw lines and stars or lines and dashes around the edges of the gift tag.

6

The Rose Gift Ensemble includes a lovely gift bag, which is a work of art in and of itself. Made from special watercolor paper, the bag is complemented by a gift tag, painted with a single rose, and a beautiful greeting card.

MATERIALS

❊ 140 lb. (63.6 g) watercolor paper, 8" x 16" (20.5 x 40.5 cm), two

❊ Watercolors: alizarin crimson, permanent magenta, yellow ochre, hooker's green, cobalt blue, burnt sienna

❊ Paintbrushes: No. 8 round, 1/2" (1.3 cm) sponge (optional)

❊ 1/4" (6 mm) emerald green velvet ribbon, 1 yd. (0.95 m)

❊ 3/8" (1 cm) pink ribbon rose

❊ 3" x 5" (7.5 x 12.5 cm) cotton lace

❊ White craft glue

❊ Acrylic matte medium (optional)

❊ Pattern sheet

❊ Miscellaneous items: fine mist spray bottle, scissors, tracing paper, graphite paper, pencil, letter opener, thick paper towels, container of water, paper punch, soft eraser

1 **Gift Bag:** Refer to the Gift Bag Guide to cut and fold the watercolor paper. Use a letter opener to crease the fold lines. Do not glue until painting is completed.

2 Trace the Gift Bag painting pattern onto tracing paper. Use graphite paper to transfer design to front and back of bag. Refer to photo and to page 158 for Painting Instructions and Techniques and for all steps below.

3 **Lacy Background:** Mix ¼ tsp. (1 mL) burnt sienna, ⅜ tsp. (1.5 mL) cobalt and ⅛ tsp. (0.5 mL) green with 3 oz. (75 g) of water in the spray bottle. Shake well to mix before each use; spray on paper towel to test color. Lay bag flat on table. Tear a thick paper towel into irregular-shaped pieces and cover the traced designs.

4 Place lace on bag. Spray lightly, holding bottle close to lace for darker values and farther away for lighter values. Move lace to another area, overlapping previous area to prevent definite lines. If area is too dark or if heavy drips fall on paper, blot lightly with paper towel.

5 **Rose:** Use crimson to paint shaded areas. Rinse paintbrush, blot on paper towel and use damp brush to pull the color to edges of petals to give dark, medium, and light values. Alternate petals to avoid painting petals next to each other. Add a touch of magenta or yellow to the tips while wet. Let dry. Mix a touch of green with a small amount of crimson, and paint dots in rose center.

6 **Rose Leaves:** Mix green and cobalt, and paint the base of the leaves and along vein lines. Rinse the brush, blot on paper towel and pull color from the veins outward to edge of the leaves. Paint each side of the leaves, leaving a thin white line down each center for the vein. Add touches of crimson on edges of some bottom leaves while they are still wet.

7 **Holly Leaves:** Use green to paint along the vein lines. Rinse brush, blot and pull the color out to the edges. Paint one side of a leaf, then the other, leaving a thin white line down the center for the vein. Mix cobalt and green; paint the holly leaf points and the edges of the top rose leaves, allowing the paint to bleed back onto wet leaf.

8 **Finishing:** Let bag dry, then refold bag; glue bottom and side as indicated. To increase the life and strength of the bag, use the sponge brush to lightly paint with a thin coat of matte medium. Do not press hard or rub. Punch holes at top of bag and begin at the front of bag to thread ribbon for handles. Tie ribbon in a bow above the painted rose, and glue ribbon rose to bow.

9 **Large Card:** Mark 7" x 10" (18 x 25.5 cm) of watercolor paper, fold on markings, crease folds with letter opener and tear along folds. Fold 7" (18 cm) edge to within ¼" (6 mm) of opposite 7" (18 cm) edge. Crease fold with letter opener.

10 Open card and place flat on table, outside facing up. Refer to Step 2 to trace and transfer Large/Cutout card pattern. Refer to the photo to paint the ribbon cobalt. Let dry. Refer to Steps 3 and 4 to paint the lacy background. Let dry. See Steps 5 through 7 to paint rose and leaves. Use a light value of crimson to paint ¼" (6 mm) edge along back inside 7" (18 cm) edge. Let dry.

11 **Small Card:** Cut 3½" x 6½" (9 x 16.3 cm) of watercolor paper. Fold so that 3½" (9 cm) edges meet; crease with letter opener. Open and place flat on table, outside facing up. Paint rose and leaves same as for large card, using Small Card pattern.

12 **Cutout Card:** Cut 3½" x 6" (9 x 15 cm) of watercolor paper. Fold so that 3½" (9 cm) edges meet; crease with letter opener. Place on table, with fold on left, outside of card facing up. Trace the Large/Cutout card pattern onto tracing paper, omitting the holly leaves. Use graphite paper to lightly transfer design to card, aligning left petal with folded edge. Refer to Steps 5 and 6 to paint rose and leaves. Cut around painted rose, being careful not to cut fold at left petal.

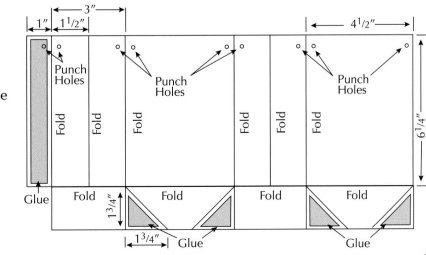

Gift Bag Guide

floral GIFT BASKET

*S*hare the Christmas spirit with someone you love by creating a floral holiday basket and filling it with gifts. After the gifts have been opened, the decorated basket can be used again. Personalize gift baskets for a tea lover, chocoholic or romantic. This one harmonizes poinsettias, pine and berries with musical ornaments and ribbon. Filled with compact discs and audio tapes, it'll be a hit with any tune-humming, foot-tapping, melody-loving music devotee!

MATERIALS

❋ White wicker vine-wrapped basket, 13″ x 8″ x 9″ (33 x 20.5 x 23 cm) with 18″ (46 cm) handle

❋ Red frosted poinsettia stems with 8″ (20.5 cm) flowers, three

❋ 20″ (51 cm) sprays, two

❋ 26½″ (67.3 cm) frosted pine branches with five 5″ (12.5 cm) sections and 2″ to 2½″ (6 to 6.5 cm) pinecones, two

❋ Green preserved hop vines, 3 oz. (75 g)

❋ 9½″ (24.3 cm) red multi-berry clusters, two

❋ 20″ (51 cm) red berry spray with eight clusters per stem, one

❋ Christmas ornaments: 8″ (20.5 cm) gold violin, one; 1½″ x 7″ (3.8 x 18 cm) gold music staff, two; 5″ (12.5 cm) sheet music rolls, two

❋ 2½″ (6.5 cm) musical print wire-edge ribbon, 2 yd. (1.85 m)

❋ Spanish moss

❋ Wire: 26-gauge green floral, 32-gauge cloth-covered

❋ Glues: white craft, hot glue gun

❋ Miscellaneous items: wire cutters, scissors

1 Left Floral Cluster: Refer to the photo for all steps below. Cut the poinsettia stems into one 12" (30.5 cm) and two 7" (8 cm) lengths. Wire the 12" (30.5 cm) poinsettia stem to the upper left of the basket handle and one 7" (8 cm) stem directly below to the handle base. Glue moss to cover poinsettia stems and left front edge of the basket.

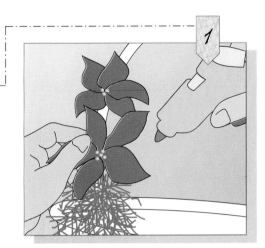

2 Cut each 20" (51 cm) pine spray into four 5" to 7" (12.5 to 18 cm) pieces. Wire and glue five surrounding the lower poinsettia, with one cascading down the basket front.

3 Cut each 26½" (67.3 cm) frosted pine branch into five 5" (12.5 cm) pieces. Wire and glue six pieces to fill in around the pine and poinsettia. Let some climb up the handle beyond the upper flower and others trail down the basket front. Glue one 9½" (24.3 cm) multi-berry cluster below the lowest poinsettia in front of the pine.

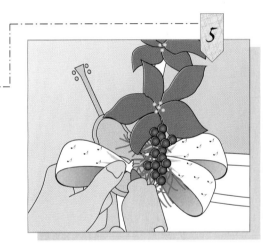

4 Glue one of each ornament to the left side of the lower poinsettia and the remaining musical staff nestled in the pine below.

5 Cut the ribbon into eight 9" (23 cm) lengths. Fold each length in half and wrap cloth-covered wire around ends to make a loop. Glue five loops in a bow-like cluster just below the lower poinsettia between the pine and berries.

6 Right Floral Cluster: Wire and glue the remaining 7" (18 cm) poinsettia stem to the right side at the handle base. Glue moss to cover the poinsettia stem and the right edge of the basket.

7 Wire and glue remaining three 5" to 7" (12.5 to 18 cm) pine pieces around the bottom edge of the poinsettia.

8 Split the remaining multi-berry cluster in half. Glue a cluster behind the top, and one below the base of the poinsettia.

9 Glue the remaining four frosted pine pieces between the pine and berries.

10 Glue the remaining ornament behind the right side of the poinsettia. Glue the remaining four ribbon loops between the pine and berries below the flower.

11 Finishing: Cut the hops into 5" to 12" (12.5 to 30.5 cm) stems. Glue the longer stems around the upper right, top and left side of the basket handle; spot-glue the tips of some hops to secure. Glue the shorter stems to fill in between the poinsettias and pine.

12 Cut the 20" (51 cm) berry spray into eight clusters. Glue them randomly around the handle and in each floral cluster.

stamped
GIFT WRAPS

$\mathcal{M}$ake your own rubber stamps, and turn plain paper and bags into one-of-a-kind gift wraps. The stamps can also be used to embellish tissue paper and ribbons. Stamps are made by cutting designs into artist's erasers or printing blocks, using a sharp mat knife. For easier cutting, select designs with simple details. Stamp pads are available at art supply stores and print shops. Some metallic inks may leave oil marks on fabric ribbons, so apply spray starch heavily to fabric ribbons and press them with an iron before stamping the designs.

MATERIALS
❋ Soft artist's eraser or printing block
❋ Tracing paper, pencil
❋ Transfer paper
❋ Mat knife
❋ Stamp pad
❋ Plain wrapping paper, tissue paper, paper bags, and ribbons as desired

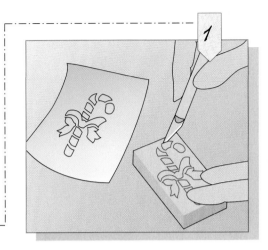

1 Trace design of your choice onto paper; for best results, keep designs simple. Transfer to smooth side of artist's eraser or printing block, using the transfer paper. Cut about ⅛" (3 mm) deep into eraser along design lines, using mat knife.

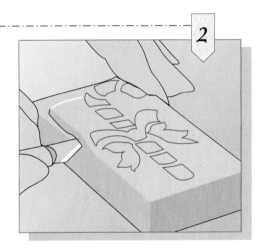

2 Remove large background area around design by cutting horizontally through the edge of eraser and up to the cuts made for the design outline.

3 Cut and remove narrow spaces within design, by cutting at an angle along each edge; remove the small background areas.

4 Press the stamp firmly onto the stamp pad; lift and repeat as necessary until the design on the stamp is evenly coated. Press stamp straight down onto paper or ribbon, using even pressure.

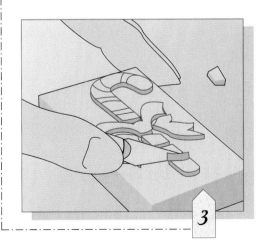

cutout WRAPPING PAPER

Give your gift a wrap that will demand

a second look by doubling up on your

wrapping paper. Cut a design or pattern into

the top layer of paper, and let the bottom

paper shine through. Depending on your

choice of paper colors and patterns, this

technique can produce a look that is natural

and earthy, or sleek and contemporary.

MATERIALS
❋ Two coordinating wrapping papers
❋ Light-colored felt-tip pen
❋ Cork-backed metal ruler
❋ Mat knife and cutting surface
❋ Aerosol adhesive (optional)
❋ Miscellaneous items: newspaper, scissors

1 Create dramatic color contrasts or subtle plays on color in your selection of wrapping papers. Shades of the same color can have a soft effect. Hot pink glowing through purple, on the other hand, is a real eye-catcher.

2 Keep patterns and designs of cutouts small, so paper folds easily around package. For a random, casual look, use a mat knife to cut freehand designs into paper.

3 Cut both wrapping papers a little larger than needed to wrap your gift. Set paper for bottom layer aside.

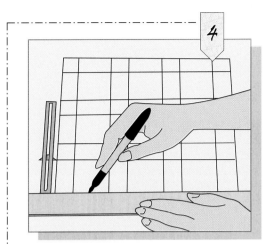

4 Mark 1" (2.5 cm) squares on the back of the paper for top layer, using a cork-backed metal ruler as a guide; space them every 2" (5 cm). Use a felt-tip pen to draw lines; don't press too hard, or impressions of the lines will show through the front of the paper. (Dark pen was used to show detail.)

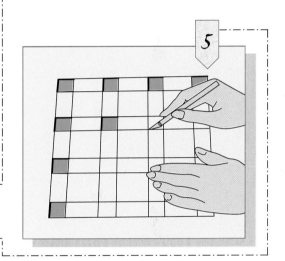

5 Place marked paper facedown on cutting surface; cut out squares, using mat knife.

6 Place cut paper facedown on newspaper. Spray with aerosol adhesive. Place paper for bottom layer facedown over adhesive so it shows through cutouts; carefully smooth out any air bubbles. Allow to dry about 15 minutes.

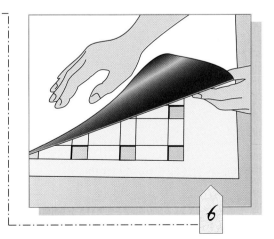

7 If you prefer not to use the aerosol adhesive, simply double-wrap the box with the cutout paper on top. Trim edges of layered paper to fit gift box, and wrap.

RIBBON GIFT-BOWS

 Packages wrapped with lavish bows make beautiful displays beneath the tree and entice the gift recipient. Ribbon gift-bows are simple to make and suitable for many types of ribbon, including wired ribbon, sinamay ribbon, paper twist and metallic twist.

MATERIALS
❋ Ribbon
❋ Hand stapler

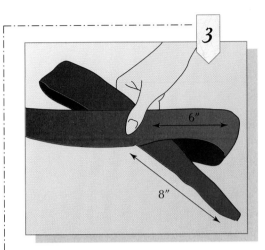

1 Wrap ribbon around box in one direction; secure with staple. Trim excess ribbon.

2 Form ribbon into a 5½" to 6" (14 to 15 cm) loop as shown, allowing about an 8" (20.5 cm) tail and taking care that the right side of the ribbon is facing out.

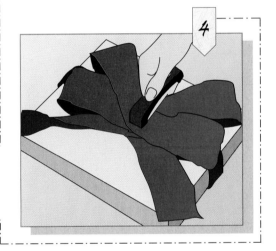

3 Fold a loop toward the opposite side, bringing ribbon over tail to keep right side of ribbon facing out.

4 Continue wrapping ribbon to form two loops on each side with a second tail extending. Position bow over ribbon on package; secure with one or two staples at center.

5 Tie about a 24" (61 cm) length of ribbon around center of bow, knotting it on back of bow. Trim tails as desired.

TECHNIQUES

General Instructions

1. Overcast the edges to prevent raveling. Fold the fabric in half vertically and horizontally to find the center, and mark it with a temporary stitch. If desired, place the fabric in an embroidery hoop. Find the center of the design by following arrows on the Chart. Count up and over to the top left stitch or specified point and begin stitching.

2. Each square on a Cross-Stitch Chart represents one square of evenweave fabric, unless otherwise indicated. Symbols correspond to the colors given in the Color Key.

3. Cut floss into 18" (46 cm) lengths. Separate the strands and use the number specified in the project. Stitching tends to twist the floss; allow the needle to hang free from your work to untwist it.

4. To begin, do not knot the floss, but hold a tail on the back of the work until anchored by the first few stitches. To carry the floss across the back to another area to be stitched, weave the floss under previously worked stitches to new area, but do not carry the floss more than three or four stitches. To end the floss, run it under several stitches on the back, then cut it. Do not use knots.

5. Work all cross-stitches first, then any additional stitches, including backstitches. Work in horizontal rows wherever possible. To make vertical stitches, complete each cross-stitch before moving to the next one.

6. When stitching is completed, wash the fabric in warm sudsy water if needed. Roll it in a terrycloth towel to remove excess moisture. Press it facedown on another terrycloth towel to dry.

Stitches

Backstitch

Up at 1, down at 2, up at 3, down at 4, stitching back to meet prior stitch.

Cross-Stitch

Work first half of each stitch left to right; complete each stitch right to left.

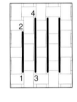

Satin-Stitch

Up at 1, down at 2, up at 3 down at 4.

Smyrna Cross-Stitch

Up at odd, down at even numbers, working in numerical sequence.

Threading Blending Filament:

Fold a length of blending filament in half; pass loop through eye of the needle.

Pull thread loop over end of needle.

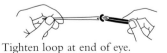

Tighten loop at end of eye.

Gently stroke knotted filament to "lock" it in place.

HARDANGER

General Instructions

Follow General Instructions for Cross-Stitch, except that you will not separate strands of pearl cotton.

Stitches

Cutting Fabric Threads

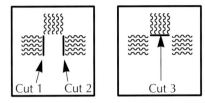

Cut along end of Kloster blocks, making cuts perpendicular to stitches.

Dove's Eye

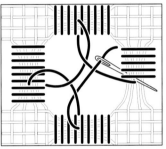

Work ½ a woven bar if only 1 side of a cutout has a woven bar, and 2½ sides if a cutout has 3 woven bars. Bring needle through center of bar or side 2 from the bottom. Go under thread loop and through center of bar or side 3; continue around square. Complete last half of woven bar.

Eyelet

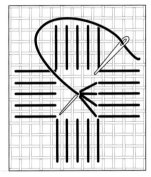

Bring needle up in center hole of block. Then work around hole from outside back to center, pulling stitch to outside to create large center hole.

Kloster Block

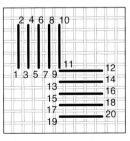

Up at 1, down at 2, up at 3, etc., to work five satin stitches over four fabric threads. To turn corner, a hole is shared by 9 and 11.

Woven Bars

Up at 1, down at 2, up at 3 over two fabric threads. Weave in a figure 8 motion (over 2, under 2) until bar is filled.

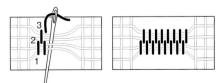

General Instructions

1. Each line on a Plastic Canvas Chart represents one bar of plastic canvas.

2. To cut plastic canvas, count the lines on the graph and cut the canvas accordingly, cutting up to, but not into the bordering bars. Follow the bold outlines where given. Use a craft knife to cut small areas.

3. To stitch, do not knot the yarn, but hold a tail in back and anchor with the first few stitches. To end yarn, weave tail under stitches on back, then cut it. Do not stitch over edge bars.

4. When finished stitching individual pieces, finish edges and join pieces as specified with an overcast stitch.

Stitches

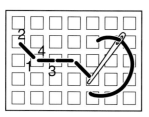

Backstitch
Up at 1, down at 2, up at 3, down at 4, stitching back to meet prior stitch.

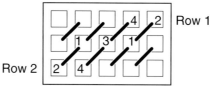

Continental Stitch
Work Row 1, up at 1, down at 2, up at 3, down at 4, working toward left. Work Row 2, up at 1, down at 2, working toward right in established sequence.

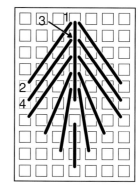

Cross-Stitch
Stitch from lower left to upper right corner, then cross back.

French Knot
Up at 1, wrap thread around needle specified number of times, down near 1.

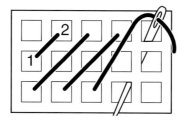

Gobelin Stitch
Up at 1, down at 2, working diagonal stitches over two or more bars in direction indicated on graph.

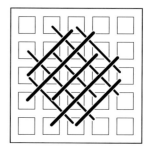

Leaf Stitch
Up at 1, down at 2, up at 3, down at 4 working counterclockwise to form leaf shape. Work long stitch over the center last.

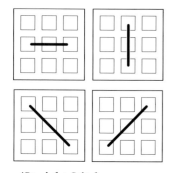

Long/Straight Stitch
Stitch over specified number of bars as indicated on graph.

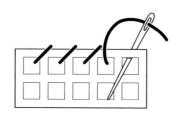

Overcast Stitch
Use a whipping motion over the outer bars to cover or join canvas edges.

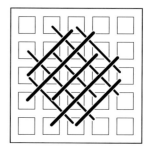

Padded Satin Stitch
Work diagonal parallel stitches in one direction. Repeat same sequence of stitches directly on top, slanting in opposite direction.

EMBROIDERY

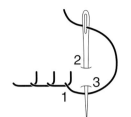

Blanket Stitch/Buttonhole
Up at 1, down at 2, up at 3 with thread below needle; pull through.

Blanket Stitch Corner 1
Make a diagonal blanket stitch. Tack stitch at corner, insert needle through loop; pull taut.

Blanket Stitch Corner 2
To work corner, use same center hole to work stitches 1, 2, and 3.

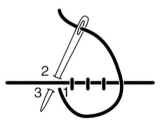

Couching Stitch
Place thread to be couched across the fabric. Up at 1, down at 2, up at 3 continuing to work tiny stitches over thread at regular intervals.

French Knot
Up at 1, wrap thread around needle specified number of times, down near 1.

Running Stitch
Up at odd, down at even numbers for specified length.

CROCHET

Abbreviations

beg . . . . .Beginning	lp(s) . . . .Loops	st(s) . . . .Stitch(es)
bet . . . . .Between	rem . . . .Remaining	tog . . . . .Together
ch . . . . .Chain	rep . . . .Repeat	tr . . . . . .Treble Crochet
dc . . . . .Double Crochet	rnd . . . . .Round	yo . . . . .Yarn Over
dec . . . .Decrease	sc . . . . .Single Crochet	★ . . . . .Repeat following
dtr . . . .Double Triple Crochet	sk . . . .Skip	instructions a given
hdc . . .Half Double Crochet	sl st . . . .Slip Stitch	number of times
inc . . . .Increase	sp(s) . . . .Space(s)	

Beginning Slip Knot
Begin with a slip knot on hook about 6" (15 cm) from end of yarn. Insert hook through loop; pull to tighten.

Chain Stitch (ch)
Yarn over, draw yarn through loop on hook to form new loop.

Decreasing in Single Crochet (dec)
1. Draw up a lp in each of next 2 sts; yo and draw yarn through all 3 lps on hook in direction of arrow.
2. 1 lp on hook.

Double Crochet (dc)
1. For first row, yarn over, insert hook into 4th chain from hook. Yarn over; draw through 2 loops on hook.
2. Yarn over and pull yarn through last 2 loops on hook.

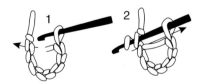

Forming Ring with a Slip Stitch
1. Insert hook in first chain.
2. Yarn over, and pull through all loops on hook.

Half Double Crochet (hdc)
1. For first row, yarn over, insert hook into 3rd chain from hook and draw up a loop.
2. Yarn over and pull through 3 loops on hook.

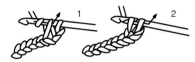

Single Crochet (sc)
1. For first row, insert hook into 2nd chain from hook and draw up a loop.
2. Yarn over and pull through both loops on hook.

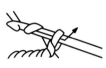

Slip Stitch (sl st)
Insert hook in stitch and draw up a loop. Yarn over and draw through both loops on hook.

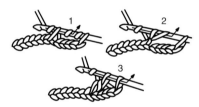

Treble Crochet (tc)
For first row, yarn over 2 times; insert hook into 5th chain from hook and draw up loop.
1. Yarn over and pull through first 2 loops on hook.
2. Yarn over and pull through 2 loops on hook.
3. Yarn over and pull through last 2 loops on hook.

Yarn Over (yo)
Wrap yarn over hook from back to front and proceed with specific stitch instructions.

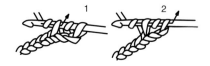

PAINTING

General Instructions

1. Sanding: Many projects are done on wood, and so must be sanded. If painting on a non-wood surface, make sure it is clean and dry. Begin the process with coarse-grit sandpaper, and end with finer grits. A 150-grit sandpaper will put finish smoothness on surfaces, such as preparing for staining or sanding. A 220-grit extra-fine sandpaper is good for smoothing stained or painted wood before varnishing, or between coats. Use a tack cloth—a treated, sticky cheesecloth—to lightly remove sanding dust after each step. Don't rub over the surface or you will leave a sticky residue on the wood. Wood files, sanding blocks and emery boards can be used to sand hard-to-reach places and curves.

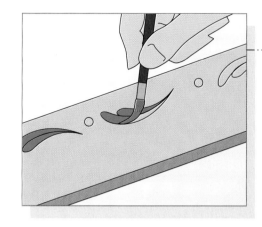

2. Transferring: Place pattern on surface or wood, following direction for grainline. For pattern outlines, such as for cutting your own pieces, use a pencil to trace around pattern piece onto wood. Trace lightly, so wood is not indented. To transfer detail lines, you can use pencil, chalk, transfer paper or graphite paper. Ink beads over many waxed transfer papers, so if you plan to use fine-line permanent-ink markers for detail lines, be sure to use graphite or wax-free transfer paper. Transfer as few lines as possible, painting freehand instead. Do not press hard, or surface many be indented. Use eraser to remove pencil lines, damp cloth on chalk, and paint thinner or soap and water on graphite.

To use pencil or chalk, rub the wrong side of traced pattern. Shake off any loose lead; lay pattern penciled or chalk-side down on wood, and retrace pattern with a pencil or stylus.

To use transfer or graphite paper, place paper facedown on wood, then place pattern on top. Lightly trace over pattern lines. Lay a piece of wax paper on top of pattern to be traced. This protects your original traced pattern and also lets you see what you have traced.

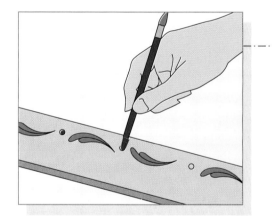

3. Brushes: The size should always correspond in size to the area being painted, preferably with the largest brush that will fit the design area. The brush should also reflect the technique being done, which is usually suggested in craft project directions.

4. Extender: Acrylic extender is a medium to add to acrylic paints to increase their open time. Open time refers to the amount of time in which you can mix and blend the paints before they begin to dry. Those familiar with oil paints are most concerned with this, or if you are doing very complex designs with a great deal of shading.

Techniques

Adding a Wash:
Dilute the paint with five parts water to one part paint (or whatever proportion is requested) and mix well. Load the brush, and blot excess paint on brush onto a paper towel. Fill in the area to be painted, giving transparent coverage. A wash can also be used for shading or highlighting large areas.

Basecoating:
Applying the first coat of paint to a prepared surface, usually covering the surface and all edges in entirety. Sometimes two coats of paint are recommended. Basecoating is usually done with a flat or sponge brush.

Double Loading:
This is the same as side loading, except two colors are loaded, one on each side of the brush. The colors gradually blend into one another in the middle of the brush.

Comma Strokes:
This is a stroke that is in the shape of a comma, with a large head and long, curvy thin tail. They come in all shapes and sizes. Begin painting up at the round head and curve down to the tail. Comma strokes require practice before they look right.

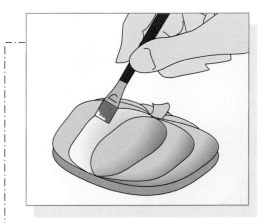

Dots:
Dots can be made by dipping the end of the paintbrush or stylus or even a toothpick in paint and then touching it gently on the painted surface. This technique can create perfect eyes or dots better than any brush tip.

Dry-Brushing:
This technique is used to achieve a soft or aged look; many times it is used to blush cheeks. Dip dry brush tips in a small amount of paint (undiluted for heavy coverage and diluted for transparent coverage). Wipe on paper towel until almost no paint is left. Then gently brush on the surface.

Highlighting:
Highlighting is the reverse of shading, causing an area to be more prominent. Thus a lighter color, such as white, is often loaded on a flat brush and used for highlighting. Highlighting is also sometimes done with a liner brush, by painting a straight line with a light color over an area to give a dimensional appearance.

Shading:
Shading is done with a color darker than the main color, making an area recede into the background. It is frequently used on edges of designs and done with the side load or floating technique. On an orange background, the brush is loaded with rust, and pulled along the edge, with the paint edge of brush where color is to be darkest.

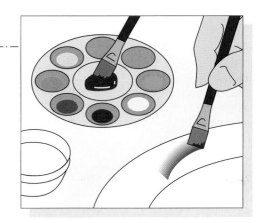

Side Loading or Floating Color:
Side loading or floating is usually done with a flat or shader brush. Dip or load brush in water; then lightly blot on paper towel to release some moisture. Load or pull one side of the brush through paint. Blend paint on a mixing surface so the color begins to move across the bristles, and is dark on one edge, but light on the other. Make sure to get the paint well blended before actually painting on the surface. Another method is to thin the paint (see below) and mix it well. Load the paint by dipping one corner in, and blending well on a mixing surface, as above.

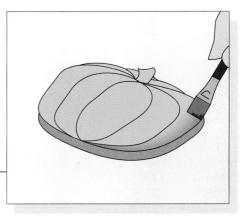

Stippling:
This is a stenciling technique, and is very similar to dry-brushing, except it gives a more fuzzy or textured look. Stencil, fabric or stippler brushes may be used, or any old scruffy brush. Dip just brush tips in a small amount of paint, then blot on paper towel until brush is almost dry. Apply the paint to the surface by pouncing up and down with the bristle tips until desired coverage is achieved.

Thinning:
Add drops of water and mix until the paint is of an inklike consistency. Sometimes a specific mix of water and paint is requested.

Sources

Page 48: *Crackled Angel*
Victorian Angel Item # 12883 by Walnut Hollow. Call 1-800-950-5101.

Page 52: *Gingerbread Birdhouse*
Large Sunny Chalet 10³/4″ birdhouse Item # 11115 by Walnut Hollow.
Call 1-800-950-5101.

Page 60: *Noel Stocking*
14″ Christmas stocking with Aida cuff by Charles Craft. Four new seasonal prints
available every year. Call 910-844-3521.

Page 80: *Drum Ornament*
Dip-N-Drape prestarched fabric, call Zim's 1-800-453-6420. Approx. $4 for
3-yd. package.

Page 92: *Sparkling Lace Ornaments.* Doilies are from Annie's collection of
crocheted doilies. Call 1-800-282-6643 for a current catalog.

Page 94: *Molded Clay Ornaments*
1-lb. packages by Creative Paperclay, 1800 So. Robertson Blvd., Suite 907,
Los Angeles, CA 90035. Call 310-839-0466.

Page 124: *Apple Checkerboard*
9″ x 12″ French corner bass wood plaque Item # 1849 by Walnut Hollow.
Call 1-800-950-5101.

Credits

DECK THE HALLS

Created by: The Editors of Creative Publishing international, Inc. in cooperation
with *Crafts Magazine* – PJS Publications Incorporated.

President: Iain Macfarlane
Executive V.P.: William B. Jones

Group Director, Book Development: Zoe Graul
Creative Director: Lisa Rosenthal
Senior Managing Editor: Elaine Perry
Senior Art Director: Stephanie Michaud
Project Editor: Deborah Howe
Copy Editor: Janice Cauley
Illustrator: Earl R. Slack
Desktop Publishing Specialist: Laurie Kristensen
Print Production Manager: Gretchen Gundersen

Editor: Judith Brossart

IBSN 0-86573-196-9

Printed on American paper by:
 World Color Press
01 00 99 98 / 6 5 4 3 2

Creative Publishing international, Inc.
offers a variety of how-to books.
For information write:
 Creative Publishing international, Inc.
 Subscriber Books
 5900 Green Oak Drive
 Minnetonka, MN 55343

*Due to differing conditions, materials and skill levels, the publisher and
various manufacturers disclaim any liability for unsatisfactory results or injury
due to improper use of tools, materials or information in this publication.*